P9-ARB-006

HOME WATERS		WHERE MARKETED		FORMS AVAILABLE IN THE AMERICAN MARKET						
MARINE (COLD)	MARINE (WARM)	NORTH AMERICA	EUROPE	WHOLE	STEAKS FILLETS	FRESH	FROZEN	COOKED	CANNED	SALTED SMOKED

© by Arthur Hawkins from The Complete Seafood Cookbook, published by Prentice-Hall, Inc.

continued on back endpapers

THE
COMPLETE
SEAFOOD
COOKBOOK

THE COMPLETE SEAFOOD COOKBOOK

BY ARTHUR HAWKINS

ILLUSTRATED BY THE AUTHOR

PRENTICE-HALL, INC.
Englewood Cliffs, New Jersey

THE COMPLETE SEAFOOD COOKBOOK
by Arthur Hawkins

© 1970 by Arthur Hawkins

Printed in the United States of America

1SBN 0-13-163105-5

Prentice-Hall International, Inc., London
Prentice-Hall of Australia, Pty. Ltd., Sydney
Prentice-Hall of Canada, Ltd., Toronto
Prentice-Hall of India Private Ltd., New Delhi
Prentice-Hall of Japan, Inc., Tokyo

For
———
Bland
Nancy
Suzie
Kathy

ACKNOWLEDGEMENTS

When I undertook this book, I realized that I was going to need lots of help.

I got it.

I got help from friendly men at the Fulton Fish Market, from fishmongers in seafood stores along Ninth Avenue in New York City, and from fishermen up and down the coast.

I got help from willing research and reference experts in the New York Public Library.

I got recipes and suggestions from helpful restauranteurs and chefs in San Juan, Madrid, Barcelona, Majorca, Baltimore, and New York (the seafood capitals of the world), and from leading restaurants of France and Italy.

I got help, cooperation, and inspiration from Jane Axt, my editor, and from Carl Koenig, production expert and gourmet.

I got help from my wife—a great cook—who advised, criticized, tasted, tested, and suggested.

Without all that help . . . no book! So to all the aforesaid people, I hereby declare my indebtedness and thanks.

INTRODUCTION

Three-fourths of the earth's surface is covered by water, and that's living quarters for a lot of seafood.* But before you go off the deep end, it should be noted that the seafood we eat comes from a very limited portion of this vast area.

The great underwater shelves surrounding the continents, depositories for food brought by rivers and streams, serve as a gastronomic gathering ground for most of the world's food fish. Inlet and bay bottoms, offshore rocks and crags harbor most of the crustacea and mollusks—the oysters and clams, lobsters and crabs, the shrimp and scallops and mussels. Inland, lakes and rivers, ponds and streams accommodate a bountiful variety of freshwater fish—trout, bass, crappie and carp; perch, pike, pickerel, and chub. . . .

The fish are there. They gather in seemingly endless quantities on the Grand Banks of Newfoundland, up and down the Atlantic and Pacific coasts of the United States, in the Alaskan and Japanese waters. They are plentiful in the waters around the British Isles, Iceland, and Norway, in the Mediterranean and in the Caribbean, and in the Gulf of Mexico, Long Island Sound, and the Chesapeake Bay.

And where the fish are, the fishermen are, too. Commercial fishing fleets of all nations trawl the gathering places, or put out dories from which the crew work with barbed and baited handlines. Lobstermen empty and rebait their pots, crabs are dredged, clams are dug, oysters are tonged, the shrimp boats are at work. The seafood is gathered from the ocean depths, bay bottoms, rivers, and lakes in nearly unbelievable variety. Yet there are still fish in the sea that man has not tasted—or caught—or even discovered. And every day we are learning to eat species we once considered inedible.

But sometimes many days lapse between catch and consumption. The catch must be preserved. It must be iced or frozen or

* There being no definitive word that embraces both freshwater and saltwater fish and shellfish, the term *seafood* will be used all-inclusively in this book.

salted and dried or smoked until it reaches the markets—or the packers—or the canneries often thousands of miles away.

And so the catch reaches the consumer in widely diverse forms —whole, dressed, filleted, sliced; shredded or flaked; iced, frozen, salted, or smoked; alive, pickled, cooked, raw; canned, packaged. . . .

How do you keep up with it all? How do you know what to buy—and how much—and how to cook it? We hope that you will find the answers to most of your questions in the pages of this book. And we hope that the recipes herein will provide you with an abundance of exciting and unusual meals.

CONTENTS

INTRODUCTION   7

1. HOW TO BUY SEAFOOD   11

   identifying fish and shellfish;
   judging freshness; forms found
   in the market; how much to buy

2. HOW TO CLEAN AND DRESS SEAFOOD   15

   scaling, cleaning, dressing, and
   filleting all kinds of fish;
   shucking oysters and clams; killing
   and cleaning lobsters, crabs, terrapin,
   and turtles; cleaning shrimp,
   prawns, mussels, squid, and octopuses

3. HOW TO PREPARE SEAFOOD   21

   frying, sautéeing, broiling, grilling,
   baking, steaming, poaching, and planking
   fish and shellfish; making fish
   forcemeat

4. SEAFOOD RECIPES   27

   appetizers
   soups, stews, chowders, bisques,
      bouillabaisse, and gumbos
   fish and shellfish entrees
   specialties
   courts-bouillons, stocks, and fumets
   sauces
   stuffings

INDEX   205

1

HOW TO BUY SEAFOOD

HOW TO BUY SEAFOOD

You don't have to possess great talent to pick out a package or two of frozen seafood for dinner. The name of the fish and all you need to know is spelled out on the package. But buying *fresh* seafood can be tricky. In the first place, if you're trying to identify fish by name, you're apt to find yourself in trouble because the fish markets of different regions don't seem to speak the same language. Scup in the North-East become porgy when you travel south. Blowfish, puffers, and sea-squab are the same fish, and so are striped bass and rockfish, dollarfish and butterfish, grouper and jewfish, rosefish, redfish, and sea perch. What's a shopper to do? You can't even tell the fish by their appearance. All flatfish seem to look alike—winter flounder, summer flounder (also called fluke, just to confuse you), starry flounder, lemon sole, and gray sole (that aren't sole at all), black-backs, yellow-tail, and dab. They're all thin, oval, surrounded by fins, and with both eyes on the same side. But they vary slightly in size, in shape, in thickness, in color, in markings, and—get this—the eyes are not always on the same side. (Can't you see yourself going to market and asking for a left-handed flounder?)

Perhaps it isn't important which of several closely related fish you buy, or what name it goes by. "A rose by any other name would smell as sweet," as the man said, but if it's fish you're buying, it better not smell at all. Well, it's got a right to smell like fish, but a strong, objectionable odor is a sure sign of deterioration. A fish that has begun to give up also gets a discouraged look in his eyes, so look for eyes that are bright and bulging. And look for gills that are reddish-pink, and scales that stick tightly to the skin, and firm elastic flesh that clings tightly to the bones. An alert buyer will have no difficulty selecting fresh seafood and a careful buyer will keep it in the coldest part of the refrigerator until time for cooking.

If it's shellfish you're buying, you'll find these, too, in a variety of forms. Lobsters and crabs (hard and soft shell) are usually available alive on ice (poke them and make them move to be sure they haven't passed on to another world), and so are oysters, clams, and mussels (pick out those with tightly closed shells, or buy them freshly shucked). In some localities you can find abalone, conch, snails, and sea urchins. Prawns and shrimp, usually sold headless, are fresh if greenish in color and firm to the touch. Scallops are always shelled and cleaned before they are marketed (in this country only the adductor muscle is eaten). Hard shell crabs, lobsters, and shrimp are sometimes steamed in the shell and sold cold. The Blue Claw crab of the East coast is also steamed, then picked and packed according to established grades (back-fin, lump, flake, and claw meat). The body meat and the claw meat of the Pacific Dungeness crabs are packed together. Almost all kinds of shellfish are available in quick-frozen packages or cans (packed in brine or smoked and packed in oil).

market forms

both frozen fish and fish kept on ice are marketed in a variety of forms, depending usually upon size. Small fish like smelt and white-bait are sold whole, but most sizes are drawn or dressed, some are filleted or cut into steaks or sticks. The following chart may prove helpful:

THE WHOLE FISH is just as it came from the water. In the market, fish sold whole are usually small and are cooked as is, or with only the entrails removed.

DRAWN FISH are marketed with only the entrails removed.

DRESSED FISH have been eviscerated and scaled, and the head, tail, and fins have been removed. Larger fish are often cut into chunks, smaller ones split along the back or belly and the backbone removed.

FISH STEAKS are cross-section slices of a large dressed fish an inch or more thick.

FISH FILLETS are the sides cut lengthwise away from the backbone. Most often the skin is removed, but sometimes the two sides are left joined by the belly skin. These are called butterfly fillets.

FISH STICKS are uniform slices cut lengthwise or crosswise from fillets or steaks.

how much to buy

in buying fresh seafood, it's easy to fool yourself when it comes to quantities. This is because of the varying amount of waste involved—head, tail, fins, bone, shell—and because of the varying richness of the different species. In general, fat fish, being richer, will go a little further. A fair rule to start with is to allow one-half pound, more or less, per person—more (about a pound) when buying whole fish, lobster, shrimp, or hard crab in the shell, and less (about one-third pound) of fillets, steaks, cleaned shrimp, or shucked oysters or crabs. The addition of stuffing or a rich sauce makes less seafood serve more.

2

HOW TO CLEAN
AND DRESS SEAFOOD

HOW TO CLEAN AND DRESS SEAFOOD

When you buy fresh fish in the market you expect that it will be cleaned, dressed, filleted, or steaked as desired. But what if you catch the fish yourself, or a friend drops by and leaves you part of his catch? Relax—cleaning fish is really quite easy and all you need is a sharp knife.

scaling fish

wash the fish in cold water, lay it on the cutting board, and with one hand grasp it firmly by the head. Holding a knife almost vertical, scrape off all the scales, working from tail to head

cleaning fish

(a) remove the entrails after cutting the entire length of the belly from the anal opening to the head. Small fish can be eviscerated through the gills

(b) remove the fins. Cut around the anal and pelvic fins and pull them loose. Cut the flesh above each side of the dorsal fin and pull the fin forward and out with the root bones (trimming with shears will not remove these roots)

(c) remove the head and pectoral fins together by cutting along the gill openings and through the backbone. If the backbone is large, snap it over the edge of the cutting board

(d) cut off the tail

(e) trim away loose ends and wash in cold, salted water to remove blood and any remaining membranes

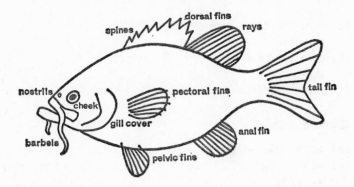

cutting fish steaks

lay the dressed fish on the cutting board and cut crosswise into one-inch slices

cutting fish fillets

(a) lay the whole fish, scaled but undressed, on its side and with a sharp knife cut down through the flesh above the back from the tail to just behind the head
(b) make a cut just behind the head from back to belly
(c) turn the knife flat and cut the flesh laterally above the backbone from just behind the head to the tail. The knife will run along the rib bones and the fillet will lift off in one piece
(d) turn the fish and repeat the operation on the other side
(e) if you wish to skin the fillets, lay them on the cutting board, skin side down, grasp the tail with your fingers, and cut through the flesh to the skin near the tail. Flatten the knife on the skin and push it forward until skin has been separated
(f) wipe the fillets with a damp cloth—do not wash

cutting fish sticks

lay the fillet on the cutting board and cut crosswise into one-inch slices

shucking oysters

(a) scrub shells well under cold running water
(b) break off the thin end or "bill" with a hammer
(c) hold oyster in palm of one hand (better wrap a cloth or towel around your hand to protect it) with the hinge toward the palm
(d) force the oyster knife between the shells at the broken end and twist
(e) slice the knife down and cut the muscle close to the upper shell
(f) slide the knife under the oyster, cutting the bottom muscle

shucking hard-shell clams

(a) scrub shells well under cold running water
(b) hold the clam in the palm of the hand with the hinge toward the palm
(c) insert strong knife between the shells, run around the clam, and twist
(d) cut the muscle holding the top shell and twist off the shell
(e) run the knife under the clam cutting the bottom muscle

cleaning hard-shell crabs

(a) drop the live crabs in a large covered pot containing about a pint of boiling water seasoned with 1/2 cup vinegar and one teaspoon cayenne pepper. Steam for 10 minutes or until shells are pink. Remove and cool
(b) break or cut off claws and legs at the body, crack and remove meat
(c) pull off the top shell from the body
(d) scrape off the whitish-colored gills from the sides
(e) remove the spongy digestive organs located in the middle of the body
(f) slice off the top of the inner skeleton beginning at the front and remove the meat from the back fin and other pockets

cleaning soft-shell crabs

(a) with a sharp knife cut off the face and eyes
(b) lift up the shell at each point and clean out the gills
(c) wash in cold running water

cleaning lobsters

(a) place live lobster on its back, insert sharp knife between body shell and tail, and cut down quickly to break spinal cord. Or plunge it head first into large pot of rapidly boiling salted water (tablespoon salt to each quart of water) for 7 minutes if less than 2 pounds, or 10 minutes if 2 pounds or more. Do not overcook
(b) with a sharp knife split the lobster open from head to tail
(c) remove the black vein running from head to tail
(d) remove the small sac back of the head

cleaning shrimp or prawns

(a) drop green shrimp in pot of salted boiling water for 5 minutes
(b) peel off shells or peel them off raw shrimp with a sharp knife
(c) remove the black vein

cleaning mussels

(a) scrub shells under cold running water
(b) drop mussels in large pot and cover with water
(c) allow to stand for 2 hours and discard all mussels that float

(d) steam in one inch of salted water for 3 minutes or until shell opens

cleaning terrapin and turtle

(a) drop the live terrapin or turtle into a pot of boiling water and simmer for 3 minutes
(b) remove, place on its back, and with a towel rub off the skin from the legs
(c) clip off the toes
(d) pull out the head and clean skin from same
(e) place into boiling water and cook until soft to the touch (about 45 minutes for a 5-inch terrapin)
(f) cool and break the shell apart
(g) carefully remove the head (and the sandbag), the gallbag (in the liver), the bones, and entrails
(h) save the meat, liver, eggs, and some of the cooking stock

cleaning squid and octopuses

(a) slit the body open, taking care not to puncture the black ink bag which should be removed. (You can save the ink and use it for making a sauce)
(b) remove the intestines, cartilage, eyes, and mouth and discard
(c) remove the tentacles. Wash
     the squid body may be stuffed or sliced
     the octopus body (and tentacles) are leathery and should be pounded until softened

3

HOW TO PREPARE SEAFOOD

HOW TO PREPARE SEAFOOD

An excellent source of digestible proteins, fats, essential minerals (calcium, phosphorus, iron, magnesium, iodine, copper), vitamins (thiamine, riboflavin, niacin, ascorbic acid, vitamins A and D), seafood is just about the most important single food available to man. It comes in all sizes and shapes, all flavors, textures, and colors. You can eat seafood for breakfast, lunch, dinner, and between meals. You can eat it dried, pickled, smoked, or raw—or you can broil it, boil it, steam it, bake it, poach it, or fry it. Tender and juicy in its raw state, just about the only thing you can do wrong with seafood is overcook it!

The principal difference in the types of seafood, as related to cooking, is the variation in fat content. As a rule, the fat fish—shad, salmon, mackerel, etc.—end up best when baked, broiled, or planked, because their high fat content keeps them from becoming dried out. Lean fish such as haddock, cod, flounder, and perch are especially suitable for steaming or poaching because the flesh is firm and will not fall apart while cooking. Both varieties do very well when fried. But actually, while these rules sound good, they can be ignored by applying a little common sense. For example, a lean fish such as halibut or sea bass will broil or bake very well if basted frequently with butter or any other fat.

So, here are the ways you can cook seafood.

deep fat frying (for fish sticks and fillets, oysters, scallops, shrimp, etc. . . .)

throughout the United States more seafood is cooked by frying than by any other method—and a large part of it is done in deep fat. No self-respecting short-order restaurant would be caught dead without a deep-fat fry kettle, usually equipped with a built-in temperature control

the principle of this form of cooking is to cover the food with some sort of protective coating and then immerse it quickly into hot oil or fat. Careful temperature control seals the food moisture in and the fat out. Insufficient heat will allow the fat to permeate the food and make it soggy; too much heat will burn the surface of the food before the inside is done through. Use a shortening that will not smoke or burn at a high temperature (400°) and will not adversely affect the flavor of the food. (All vegetable shortenings, liquid or solid, are suitable—in some countries olive oil or coconut oil are used—but butter used alone, having a low smoking point, is unsatisfactory.) Here's the procedure:

1. dip the seafood into milk or a milk-egg mixture, and then into bread crumbs, cracker crumbs, flour, corn meal, or a combination of these
2. place into a wire frying basket a few pieces at a time
3. immerse into deep fat (using a thermometer) and cook until golden brown. Drain and serve at once

deep-fat fried seafood, properly cooked at the proper temperature in fresh fat, is nutritious, healthful, and digestible. Observe the rules of temperature and timing set out in the chart herewith

DEEP-FAT COOKING CHART

		Time in Minutes	
Seafood	*Temperature*	*Fresh*	*Frozen*
abalone	375°	3–5	4–6
fish fillets	365°	3–5	4–6
fish sticks	375°	3–5	4–6
oysters	365°	2–4	3–5
scallops (sea)	365°	2–4	4–6
scallops (bay)	365°	2–3	3–4
shrimp, prawns	365°	3–5	4–6
smelt	365°	2–4	4–6
soft clams	350°	2–3	—
white bait, tiny shrimp	350°	2–3	—

pan frying (for small fish, fillets, oysters, etc. . . . .)

this is the method used most often by campers cooking their fresh catch of brook trout, bass, crappie, sunfish, etc. . . . And back home in the kitchen it's the most popular method for cooking most of the fillets, fish sticks, or small fish you get from the market

1. dip the seafood into milk or a milk-egg mixture and then into bread crumbs, cracker crumbs, flour, corn meal, or a combination of these
2. cover the bottom of a heavy skillet with 1/4 to 1/2 inch of shortening or a fat-butter mixture
3. get the fat as hot as you can. As soon as it begins to smoke it's at the right temperature
4. fry the seafood 3 to 5 minutes or until golden
5. turn and fry on the other side

sautéeing (for fillets, steaks, soft-shell crabs, larger fish cut into cubes, etc. . . .)

the French refer to this method as cooking *à la meunière* and they use it for preparing small delicately-flavored fish or slices of larger ones:

1. season the seafood with salt (and herbs, if desired) and sprinkle lightly with flour
2. place into skillet with very hot butter and brown
3. turn and brown on the other side

baking

line a greased baking dish with aluminum foil very well greased (or the fish might take on a metallic flavor) allowing the ends of the foil to overlap. Place the fish with its sauces or seasonings on the foil and cook in a preheated 350° oven until it flakes when forktested. Remove by using the foil ends as handles and the fish will not break or crumble

broiling (*grilling*)   (for whole split dressed fish, for steaks, lobster, etc. . . .)

this method is suitable for almost all seafood except the smaller fish. Naturally dry fish should be brushed well with butter or a good oil to keep them from drying out. Whole fish should be gashed lightly with a sharp knife, lengthwise and across, to insure that the flesh is cooked through. Large fish should be split. Smaller fish may be pan-broiled on top of the stove. The fish will have more flavor and will be juicier if the backbone is left in

1. preheat the broiling compartment to 550°F.
2. oil the fish well (unless it is naturally oily) and dust lightly with flour
3. place it on a greased broiling rack and slide it under the flame 2 to 6 inches away depending upon thickness
4. broil for 5 to 8 minutes or until slightly brown, basting with melted butter if it is a dry fish
5. turn and repeat the procedure
6. season, garnish, and serve hot

steaming (for almost any kind of fish, shrimp, clams, crabs, oysters, etc. . . .)

here is, without a doubt, the best way to preserve the true natural flavor of seafood. A large covered pot of steaming water provides the moisture and a steaming rack prevents the seafood from touching the water and becoming soggy. All the natural juices are retained instead of being boiled out

1. the fish, if it has a tendency to flake or fall apart when cooked, is tied in cheesecloth to keep it in one piece. Clams, oysters, or shrimp can also be contained in cheesecloth and more than one kind of seafood can be steamed in the same pot at the same time
2. place a metal rack, wire basket, or other device into the pot and add 2 inches of water
3. bring the water to a boil, place the seafood in the rack, taking care that it does not touch the water, and cover tightly
4. steam any fish less than 2 inches thick about one minute per ounce. Clams or mussels are done when they're open—shrimp, lobsters, or crabs when they turn pink
5. mustard, garlic, onions, cloves, celery, herbs, and/or wine or vinegar may be added to the water, if desired. Crabs are steamed over a mixture of water, dry mustard, cayenne, black pepper, and vinegar. Clams over water alone

poaching (best suited for fish fillets, such as flounder, sole, turbot, dab, but also works well with any non-oily fish)

the fish can be poached in almost any liquid—milk, cream, white wine, fish stock, salted water, or a specially prepared *Court Bouillon* or *Fumet* (see index). When the fish has been cooked, the liquid can then be used as the basis for the sauce

There are two methods of poaching. Here's one:

1. fill a frying pan 1 inch deep with poaching liquid and heat on top of the stove to just below boiling
2. add the fillets and cook gently without boiling until they flake when tested with a fork. If the fillets are large, cut them in two to make handling easier. If they are thin, fold them
3. remove them carefully and keep them warm, while preparing the desired sauce

Or try this one:

1. place the fish in a baking tray or roasting pan that has been well buttered (or wrap it in gauze to prevent it from breaking up)

2. almost cover it with a court bouillon or fumet
3. cover the pan and place it into a preheated moderate oven of about 350°F. until the fish flakes when tested with a fork
4. remove the fish carefully with a slotted spatula to a preheated platter and keep warm until the sauce has been prepared

planking (for almost any variety of whole dressed fish or fish steak suitable for baking or broiling)

use a hardwood plank about 1 1/2 inches thick—hickory, oak, or ash—that has been well oiled. Have on hand a supply of just-undercooked vegetables (peas, carrots, cauliflower, tomatoes, etc. . . .) and hot mashed potatoes

1. place the plank in a cold oven and turn to 400°F.
2. when oven is hot, remove the plank and oil or butter it well
3. arrange the fish in the center, return to the oven and bake about 10 minutes to the pound
4. remove from the oven, arrange a border of the vegetables and hot mashed potatoes around the fish
5. return to the oven and cook until fish flakes when tested with a fork and potatoes are slightly browned

preparing fish forcemeats

forcemeats are a mixture of minced, chopped, or ground ingredients, appropriately seasoned or spiced, used principally for making stuffings. In the United States, forcemeats are commonly made from meats and end up as sauages, bolognas, salamis, patés, aspics, galantines, etc. But an important part of French cooking includes fish forcemeat which is used for stuffing seafood or making fish mousse or quenelles (fish dumplings)

the best fish for forcemeat is pike, flounder, trout, whiting, sole, carp, or other white-fleshed fish. Take two pounds of such fish (raw, skin and bones removed) and pound in a mortar until very fine, adding one teaspoon salt, 1/4 teaspoon white pepper, and a pinch of grated nutmeg during the process. Bind together by adding, gradually, the whites of 4 eggs. Force the mixture through a fine sieve and refrigerate for 2 hours. Using a spatula or wooden spoon, stir in 4 cups heavy cream until mixture is smooth

set aside for use in making quenelles, mousses, or for use as stuffing

4

SEAFOOD RECIPES

APPETIZERS

Appetizers—tidbits to whet the appetite and prepare the stomach for the meal to come—may be served hot or cold, with cocktails before the meal (snacks or canapés), or as a first course of the dinner itself (hors d'oeuvres).

When served with drinks, only those appetizers that can be eaten with the fingers make sense, in which case the seafood can be presented on toast or crackers, with toothpicks, or as a dip. The toast or crackers must be fresh and crisp, preferably hot—there is no excuse for soggy canapés.

These days, there are many prepared spreads and dips on the market which make the host's job easy, but for those who would like to be more adventurous, here are some very special appetizers you will be proud to serve.

ANCHOVY TOAST

melt 3 tablespoons butter over low heat, add 2 egg yolks, and beat with a whisk or wooden spoon. add 3 tablespoons anchovy paste, 2 tablespoons brandy, and a few grains cayenne. spread onto toast squares and serve cold

(yields 24 canapés)

CLAM SPREAD

mix together an 8-ounce package cream cheese, 1 tablespoon Worcestershire sauce, 1/2 clove garlic, minced, 2 tablespoons dry sauterne or dry vermouth, 1 tablespoon clam juice, and a little salt. add an 8-ounce can minced clams. serve on toast squares or crackers, or add a little extra clam juice and use as a dip

---

CRABMEAT BALLS

combine 1 cup crabmeat or tuna flakes (cooked or canned) with a mixture consisting of 1/4 cup mayonnaise, 1/2 teaspoon dry mustard, 1 teaspoon horseradish, a dash Worcestershire sauce, and 2 teaspoons sherry. form into marble-sized balls, bind with raw egg yolk, sprinkle with grated hard-cooked egg yolk, and serve on toothpicks

(yields about 24 balls)

CRAB LOUIS

1 head lettuce, shredded 1/2 teaspoon salt 1 pound cooked crabmeat 4 tomatoes, sliced 1 cucumber, sliced 3 hard-cooked eggs, sliced 1 cup mayonnaise 1/4 cup chili sauce 2 tablespoons chopped chives 1 tablespoon lemon juice dash Worcestershire sauce capers	place the lettuce in a large chilled salad bowl, sprinkle with salt, mound the crabmeat in the center and surround with tomato, cucumber, and egg slices combine the remaining ingredients, spoon over the crabmeat, and garnish with capers. or try this: split two avocados, remove the skin and seeds, brush with olive oil, and spoon crabmeat into them (4 servings)

HOT BUTTERED CRABMEAT CANAPÉS

melt 2 tablespoons butter in a heavy skillet and add the juice of 1/2 lemon. add 1 pound frozen lump or back fin crabmeat and sauté for a few minutes. pour in 1 ounce of cognac and season to taste with salt and cayenne pepper. serve on hot buttered toast quarters garnished with paprika

(6 servings)

EELS IN HERB SAUCE

Craig Claiborne, the *New York Times'* gustatory authority, says that this superb dish is served at the Quo Vadis in New York. I found it also at the Brussels.

sauté a pound of eels, cleaned, skinned, and cut into 1-inch pieces in 1/2 cup olive oil with 1 clove of garlic for 5 minutes. pour in 1 pint fish stock, cook 5 minutes longer and drain. add 1 cup dry white wine, 2 tablespoons lemon juice, 1/4 cup chopped parsley, 1/4 cup chopped spinach, 1/4 cup chopped chives or scallions, a little chopped mint, and season to taste with salt and freshly ground pepper. mix well, cook for 5 minutes, chill and serve

(6 servings)

FINNAN HADDIE SNACKS

melt 4 tablespoons butter in the top section of a double boiler, stir in 2 teaspoons flour, add 2 teaspoons finely chopped onion, and 4 tablespoons chopped mushrooms. cook for a few minutes, then add 2 egg yolks previously lightly beaten with 1/2 cup cream and 3 tablespoons grated cheese. stir and add 1 cup cooked flaked finnan haddie, season to taste with salt and cayenne and cook for a minute or so. place on quartered slices of toast and brown on a cookie sheet under the broiler. serve hot

you can substitute kippers or sardines for finnan haddie

(yields 24 canapés)

HERRING DIP

mince 3 pickled herrings and mix with 1 tablespoon mustard, 1 teaspoon horseradish, a dash Worcestershire sauce, a dash Tabasco, and a few drops lemon juice. fold in 1/2 cup heavy cream, whipped, or 1/2 cup sour cream

KIPPER SNACKS

melt 2 tablespoons butter in the top section of a double boiler, add 1/2 cup cream, 1 tablespoon Worcestershire sauce, and 2 tablespoons of grated sharp cheese. stir until thickened and spoon over quartered slices of toast on which have been placed strips of canned kippered herrings and quarter-slices of cooked bacon. place on a cookie sheet and brown quickly under the broiler. serve hot

(yields 24 canapés)

LOBSTER SPREAD

to 1 cup finely chopped lobster meat add the yolks of 4 hard-cooked eggs, well mashed, 2 tablespoons melted butter, and 4 tablespoons heavy sweet (or sour) cream. season to taste with salt, pepper, dry mustard, and a few drops Worcestershire sauce. mix well. you can substitute finely chopped shrimp, crabmeat, tuna, or almost any other fish or shellfish

(yields 2 cups)

MUSSEL TIDBITS

take the meat from mussel shells, remove the beards, roll in 2-inch bacon strips, and fasten with toothpicks. arrange rolls in a shallow baking pan, sprinkle with paprika, and broil for 2 minutes (or until bacon is crisp) in a preheated 450° oven. serve hot

HOT LOBSTER CANAPÉS

to 1 cup chopped lobster meat add 6 ripe olives, chopped, and 2 tablespoons heavy sweet (or sour) cream. season to taste with salt, cayenne, and a dash Worcestershire sauce, place on slices of toast, quartered, and brown for a minute or so on a cookie sheet under the broiler. serve hot

you can substitute chopped shrimp, crabmeat, tuna, or almost any other fish or shellfish—or try the same recipe using minced chives and pimientos or stuffed green olives in place of ripe olives

(yields 24 canapés)

FLAKED ROCKFISH

here's a recipe—and a good one—that you can use for almost any flaked left-over fish—or even canned tuna or crabmeat

2 tablespoons butter
2 tablespoons flour
dash Tabasco
3/4 cup fish stock (see index)
3/4 cup light cream
3/4 cup flaked cooked rockfish
2 egg yolks, beaten
6 slices buttered toast, cut into strips
2 tablespoons chopped parsley

melt the butter, stir in the flour, add the Tabasco, stock, and cream, cook, stirring, over low heat until smooth and thickened

stir in the fish flakes and egg yolks and cook until desired consistency is reached

spread onto toast strips, garnish with parsley, and serve

(yields canapés for 6)

SMOKED SALMON

a prized delicacy on both sides of the Atlantic, smoked salmon is available canned or in bulk by the pound. In the United States and Canada, the top quality fish comes from Nova Scotia—in Europe, from Scotland, Norway, and Denmark

quality smoked salmon is usually sold in thin slices and is served cold on chilled plates accompanied by lemon wedges, buttered thin slices of pumpernickel or rye bread, toasted or cold, and freshly ground pepper

DEVILED SARDINES

mix the oil from 2 cans small sardines with 3 tablespoons Dijon mustard. cover the sardines with this mixture, roll them in breadcrumbs, brown under the broiler, squeeze a drop of lemon juice on each, and serve on toothpicks

(4 servings)

SARDINE SNACKS

melt 1/4 pound butter and stir in 1 crushed clove of garlic. brush or spread this mixture onto toast and cut into sardine-size strips. sprinkle sardines with a few drops of dry sauterne or dry vermouth, let stand for 15 minutes and place one on each toast strip. top with a little chopped hard-cooked egg or crisp bacon and season with a drop of lemon juice and a little salt

SEAFOOD HORS D'OEUVRES PLATTER

arrange a large platter with a variety of cold seafoods such as anchovies, smoked salmon, sardines, herring, tuna fish, shrimp, lobster salad, crab claws, etc. . . . decorate with anchovy hearts, tomato slices, raw carrot slivers, celery, scallions, parsley, watercress, etc. . . . add hard-cooked eggs, quartered, and small saucers of tartar sauce, cocktail sauce, mayonnaise, etc. . . . serve with melba toast, toasted crackers, etc. . . .

SHRIMP CANAPÉS

mix together an 8-ounce package cream cheese, 2 teaspoons curry powder, 1/2 teaspoon salt, and 4 tablespoons dry red wine. spoon this mixture onto 24 toast quarters and top each with a split cooked shrimp. serve cold with a dash of paprika and a drop of lemon juice on each

(yields 24 canapés)

CHEDDAR-TUNA CANAPÉS

mix together 1 cup flaked tuna fish, 2 cups grated Cheddar cheese, 2 tablespoons dry vermouth and a little freshly ground pepper. spread on toast quarters and place in a preheated 350° oven for a few minutes. serve hot

(yields 24 canapés)

Chicken stock is a good poaching liquid for fish if the fat is removed (chill it and skim).

Never poach fish longer than 6 minutes. The fish is done when it has lost its translucency and is firm to the touch.

SOUPS, STEWS, CHOWDERS, BISQUES, BOUILLABAISSE, AND GUMBOS

These wonderful concoctions all have one thing in common—they are in a large measure, liquid dishes. Otherwise they are so different (*vive la différence!*) and yet so similar (*vive le semblance!* too) that it seems worth while to go to the dictionary for a close-up view of the facts. Here's what you'll discover:
   soup, n. a liquid food made from meat, fish, or vegetables with various added ingredients, by boiling.
   stew, n. a preparation of meat, fish, or other food cooked by stewing (simmering or slow boiling).
   chow-der, n. a kind of soup or stew made of clams, fish, or vegetables, with potatoes, onions, other ingredients and seasoning.
   bisque, n. any smooth, creamy soup—a thick soup made of shellfish or game stewed long and slowly.
   bouil-la-baisse, n. a kind of stew or chowder made of fish and vegetables.
   gum-bo, n. a soup thickened with the mucilaginous pods of the okra.

Seafood, perhaps because of the liquid environment in which it spends its life, is more suitable than almost any other food for making into soups, chowders and the like. And now thanks to deep-freezing techniques, great varieties of shellfish, mollusks, freshwater and marine fish, once available only in or near their own habitat, are in plentiful supply all over the world.

Cooks who have longed for a change of pace in seafood fare never had it so good! In many of the recipes that follow, a venturous or creative cook will find it easy to substitute one form of seafood for another.

CLAM BROTH

clam broth can be used to flavor other seafood dishes or served hot as a soup. or you can chill it, mix with tomato juice or chili sauce and serve as a cocktail. it's easy to make. all you do is scrub the clams (any kind) and put them into a pot with 1/2 cup water, cover tightly, steam for 1/2 hour, and strain

CLAM BELLY SOUP

here is a superb soup I discovered at Gage & Tollner's, a gaslight restaurant that has been on Fulton Street in Brooklyn since 1879—and that's old even for Brooklyn. This soup made from the round soft parts—the bellies—of soft clams is so delicately subtle that even my wife (who is no clam buff by any means) fell for it hook, line, and sinker

2 dozen soft clams **2 cups light cream** **2 tablespoons butter** **pinch nutmeg** **dash salt** **1 teaspoon sherry**	scrub the clams and steam them in a little water until the shells open remove the soft round bellies, discarding the necks and other parts to a little of the strained broth from the steaming add the cream, butter, and seasoning simmer two minutes, add the clam bellies and sherry. simmer 1 minute and serve (2 servings)

DELAWARE CRAB SOUP

2 tablespoons butter
1 tablespoon flour
2 cups water
1/2 pound crabmeat, fresh or canned
1 onion, chopped
1 stalk celery, chopped
1 sprig parsley, chopped
pinch thyme
dash Tabasco
pinch salt
dash pepper
3 cups milk, scalded

melt the butter, brown the flour, stir in the water, and add the crabmeat, vegetables, and seasonings. simmer for half an hour

pour in the hot milk, check seasoning and serve

(4 servings)

CRAB SOUP WITH BEER

1/2 pound fresh or canned crabmeat
1 can tomato soup
1 can pea soup
1 can beer
1 cup milk
1 dash Worcestershire sauce
salt and pepper

put all the ingredients into a pot and heat. do not boil

check seasoning and serve

(4 servings)

SHE CRAB SOUP

here is a very old recipe from Charleston, South Carolina. I've never made this soup exactly according to recipe—too lazy, I guess, to pick the crabs—then, too, I couldn't get female crabs at the time I wanted to make the soup. (the eggs in the "she" crab are reputed to give an extra exotic flavor.) make it the way I did, using 1/2 pound of fresh, cooked crabmeat or try your hand with the original recipe

1 dozen "she" crabs
1 tablespoon butter
1 small onion
salt and pepper
2 cups milk, scalded
1/2 cup cream
1/2 teaspoon
Worcestershire sauce
1 tablespoon flour blended
with 1 tablespoon butter
1 tablespoon sherry wine

cook the crabs until tender in boiling salted water (about 20 minutes). pick the meat from the shells and put it, along with the crab eggs, into the top of a double boiler with the butter, onion, salt, and pepper simmer for 5 minutes and stir in the milk. add the cream and Worcestershire

thicken with the flour-butter roux, add the sherry, and simmer for half an hour. check seasoning and serve

(4 servings)

LOBSTER SOUP

2 tablespoons butter
1/2 cup mushrooms,
chopped
1 onion, chopped
2 sprigs parsley, chopped
1 clove garlic, crushed
1 bay leaf
1/2 teaspoon allspice
1/2 pound cooked ham,
minced
1 tablespoon flour blended
with 1 tablespoon butter
1/2 cup canned tomatoes
1 cup hot water
1/2 pound fresh or frozen
lobster meat, coarsely
chopped
2 hard-cooked eggs,
chopped
salt and pepper
2 tablespoons sherry wine

place 2 tablespoons of butter, the mushrooms, onion, parsley, garlic, bay leaf, allspice, and ham into a large pot and sauté gently for 10 minutes

add the flour and butter, stirring, and then the tomatoes and hot water. cover and simmer 15 minutes

add the lobster meat and chopped eggs. heat well but do not boil

season to taste, stir in the sherry wine, and serve

(4 servings)

SOFT-SHELL CRAB SOUP

1/2 cup olive oil
2 onions, chopped
2 leeks (white parts only), chopped
1 clove garlic, crushed
1 can tomatoes
1 pint dry white wine
1 cup hot water
salt and pepper
cayenne
6 soft-shell crabs (4, if large), cleaned (see index)
2 pounds fish fillets (haddock, red snapper, whiting, etc.) cut into pieces, if large
1/4 pound thin spaghetti

heat the oil in a large pot, sauté the onions until golden and toss in the leeks, garlic, and tomatoes

add the wine, water, and seasonings and bring to a boil

add the crabs, cover and simmer 15 minutes

add the fillets and simmer 15 minutes longer

remove the crabs and fish to a heated, covered dish

put the spaghetti into the broth and boil to desired tenderness

serve the soup and seafood together—or as separate courses

(4 generous servings)

COLD SHRIMP SOUP

1 pound cooked shrimp, finely chopped
1 tomato, peeled and finely chopped
1 cucumber, peeled and finely chopped
2 cups canned chicken bouillon
2 cups sour cream
2 tablespoons fresh dill (or chives), finely chopped
salt and pepper

mix everything together thoroughly and season to taste

chill and serve garnished with fresh dill or chives

(4 servings)

MUSSEL SOUP

2 quarts mussels, well
scrubbed
1/2 cup dry white wine
3 teaspoons parsley,
chopped
pinch thyme
dash cayenne
1/4 pound butter
4 shallots (or spring
onions), finely chopped
1 clove garlic, finely
chopped
2 cups hot water
1 cup milk, scalded
2 egg yolks, beaten
1/2 cup cream
1 teaspoon lemon juice
salt and pepper

put the mussels into a pot with the wine, parsley, thyme, and cayenne, and cook until shells open. strain the broth, remove the mussels from their shells, set the mussels aside and discard the shells

sauté the shallots and garlic in the butter until golden. add the water, mussel broth, and then the milk. simmer for 10 minutes

add the mussels

mix the egg yolks, cream, and lemon juice and stir into the soup, heat again, and season to taste

(4 servings)

SHRIMP SOUP

2 tablespoons butter
1 onion, chopped
1/4 cup flour
4 cups milk
1 pound cooked shrimp,
finely chopped
2 stalks celery, finely
chopped
1 teaspoon
Worcestershire sauce
dash Tabasco sauce
salt and pepper
1 cup cream
2 tablespoons sherry wine

sauté the onion in the butter until golden

stir in the flour and gradually add the milk. simmer gently

add the shrimp, celery, Worcestershire and Tabasco, continuing to simmer

season to taste with salt and pepper, then add the cream and sherry wine. heat but do not boil

(4 servings)

CHARLESTON OYSTER SOUP

1 tablespoon butter mixed
with 1 tablespoon flour
1/2 cup cream
pinch nutmeg
pinch mace
salt and pepper
2 cups water
1 dozen oysters (more if
small), with their liquor

put the oyster liquor into a
saucepan, bring it almost to a
boil and skim

add the butter-flour mixture,
cream, and seasonings. bring
again almost to a boil, add 2
cups water, and simmer until
slightly thickened

add the oysters. serve as soon
as the edges begin to curl

you'll like the unusual flavor
the mace gives

(2 servings)

OYSTER SOUP BELGIQUE

1/8 pound salt pork, finely
diced
2 medium potatoes, peeled,
boiled, and mashed
1 pint milk, scalded
1 small bouquet garni (a bay
leaf, little thyme, and
parsley tied in gauze)
1 dozen oysters (more if
small), with their liquor
salt and pepper
2 slices French bread,
toasted and buttered

cook the salt pork slowly in a
saucepan until the scraps are
crisp. remove them and set
aside

in the same saucepan place
the mashed potatoes and then
gradually add the hot milk

add the *bouquet,* bring almost
to a boil, then add the oysters
and liquor

when the oysters begin to curl
around the edges, remove and
discard the *bouquet.* season,
and serve on toasted French
bread. top with the crisp salt
pork scraps

(2 servings)

NEW ORLEANS OYSTER SOUP

1 small stalk celery, chopped
1 dozen oysters (more if small), with their liquor
1 pint milk, scalded
1 tablespoon butter blended with 1 tablespoon flour
salt and pepper
minced parsley

simmer the chopped celery in 1/2 pint of water for half an hour, toss in the oysters with their liquor, and stew gently for about 5 minutes

remove the oysters, chop them, return them to the pot, and add the hot milk

add the butter-flour mixture, stir, simmer, season, and serve garnished with parsley

(2 servings)

OYSTER SOUP VELOUTÉ

2 dozen oysters (more if small), with their liquor
2 cups water
6 tablespoons butter blended with 6 tablespoons flour
1/4 teaspoon Tabasco
salt
1 cup cream

put the oysters with their liquor into a saucepan, add 2 cups of water, bring almost to a boil, and simmer gently until the edges of the oysters have begun to curl (about a minute). remove the oysters and set aside

gradually combine the soup with the butter-flour mixture, stirring until sauce is thick and smooth. season to taste with salt and Tabasco sauce, continuing to simmer for about 20 minutes

add the cream and the oysters

simmer about 2 minutes longer and serve

(4 servings)

STEWS

Seafood stew is a healthful and satisfying dish—especially on a cold winter day. Easy to prepare, it is none the less tricky because of the danger of curdling. Milk, the principal ingredient, is a colloidal substance and its stability is affected by the indelicate application of heat or salt. And you can hardly make seafood stew without heat or without delicious, nutritious, salty seafood!

There are many procedures for making a stew, all aimed at preventing coagulation or curdling—some involving the use of special steam cookers, others using double boilers or two saucepans, but none of them will save the stew if you are careless.

If oysters are out of season or if you prefer clams, just make the substitution and proceed in exactly the same way.

OLD FASHIONED OYSTER (OR CLAM) STEW

1 dozen oysters or cherrystone clams (chop the clams if you wish)
2 tablespoons butter
1 pint milk (a little added cream will make it richer)
salt and pepper
minced parsley

melt the butter in a saucepan (or in the top of a double boiler) and add the oysters or clams (take a chance and add a little of the liquor—but too much will curdle it). simmer very gently for about 3 minutes or until the edges curl

meanwhile, in a separate saucepan, slowly heat the milk. do not boil

slowly add the contents of the second saucepan to that of the first, stirring all the time

season and serve garnished with parsley

(2 servings)

GRAND CENTRAL OYSTER BAR OYSTER
(OR CLAM) STEW

2 tablespoons butter
1 teaspoon
Worcestershire sauce
1 teaspoon paprika
1/2 teaspoon pepper
1/2 teaspoon celery salt
1 dozen medium-sized
oysters or cherrystone
clams (chop the clams if
you wish)
1 cup oyster liquor and
clam juice combined
1 pint milk, half-and-half,
or cream, as desired
butter
paprika

get the top of a double boiler as hot as possible without letting the top pan touch the water in the bottom pan. put in the butter, Worcestershire, paprika, pepper, and celery salt

stir in the oysters or clams, let them froth for half a minute, then pour in the clam broth and boil hard for half a minute longer

add the milk, half-and-half or cream, bring to the boiling point, pour into bowls, add a pat of butter, a dash of paprika, and serve

done right it doesn't curdle, but don't ask me why

(2 servings)

GRAND CENTRAL OYSTER BAR OYSTER
(OR CLAM) PAN ROAST

2 tablespoons butter
1 teaspoon
Worcestershire sauce
1 teaspoon paprika
1 dozen medium-sized
oysters or cherrystone
clams (chop the clams if
you wish)
1/2 cup clam juice
2 tablespoons chili sauce
1 cup cream
1 teaspoon lemon juice
2 slices dry toast

get the top of a double boiler as hot as possible without letting the top pan touch the water in the bottom pan. put in the butter, Worcestershire, paprika, and oysters or clams and let it froth for half a minute

pour in the clam broth, add the chili sauce, boil, and stir for half a minute

add the cream and then the lemon juice. stir for half a minute and serve on dry toast

(2 servings)

CLAM STEW, AU NATUREL

here is a warming and exhilarating dish for a cold day, especially concocted for waistline-watchers

1 tablespoon butter
1 teaspoon
Worcestershire sauce
1 teaspoon paprika
1/2 teaspoon celery salt
1 dozen cherrystone clams
(chopped, if you wish)
2 1/2 cups fresh clam juice
(or canned clam broth)

put all the ingredients into a saucepan and bring to a quick boil. reduce the heat, simmer for minute or so, and serve

(2 servings)

SOFT CLAM STEW

scrub 2 dozen soft clams and steam them quickly in a covered pot containing 1/2 cup of water. When the shells have opened, remove the clams, separate out the bellies, discarding the necks and other parts, and proceed with the stew as you would with cherrystones or oysters

SCALLOP STEW

1 tablespoon butter
1 pint fresh scallops, cleaned (and coarsely diced if they're too large)
3 cups milk, half-and-half, or cream
salt and pepper
paprika or chopped parsley

in a large saucepan, melt the butter and sauté the scallops not longer than 5 minutes (cooking too long will make them tough)

add the milk, bring almost to a boil, then simmer slowly for about 10 minutes

season to taste and serve garnished with paprika or parsley
(4 servings)

SHRIMP STEW

1 tablespoon butter
2 teaspoons flour
3 cup milk
1/4 cup chopped celery
2 cups peeled raw shrimp (fresh or frozen)
salt and pepper

in the top of a double boiler melt the butter and stir in the flour, then cook for a minute or so

stir in the milk and then the celery. simmer at a low temperature until thickened, then add the shrimp, and continue cooking for 10 minutes

season to taste and serve
(4 servings)

CODFISH STEW

1 pound fresh or frozen cod fillets **2 tablespoons butter** **1 bay leaf** **1 slice onion, finely chopped** **1 teaspoon paprika** **1 teaspoon Worcestershire sauce** **1 cup clam broth** **3 cups milk** **salt and pepper**	steam the fillets (see index), flake into pieces with a fork, and set aside meanwhile melt the butter in the top of a double boiler, add the bay leaf, onion, paprika, Worcestershire, and then the clam broth. bring to a quick boil and pour in the milk add the flaked cod, bring almost to a boil, season to taste, and serve (4 servings)

CHOWDERS

ABALONE CHOWDER

1 pound abalone meat, trimmed and pounded **1 quart water** **1 pinch thyme** **dash of Tabasco sauce** **1 teaspoon salt** **1/4 pound salt pork, diced** **1 onion, chopped** **3 potatoes, peeled and cubed** **2 cups milk or half-and-half** **3 tablespoons butter** **chopped parsley**	put the abalone into a pot of water, season with thyme, Tabasco, and salt. cover and boil for an hour or longer until it is tender. remove abalone from broth and chop meanwhile, in a skillet, sauté the salt pork and onion until crisp and golden put the abalone, salt pork, and onion into the broth, add the potatoes, and simmer 20 minutes or until potatoes are cooked stir in the milk or half-and-half, add the butter, check the seasoning, and serve garnished with chopped parsley (4 servings)

MANHATTAN CLAM CHOWDER

1/4 pound salt pork, diced
1 onion, chopped
1 cup cubed potatoes
2 cups canned tomatoes
1 pint chowder clams, finely chopped (or canned clams)
1/4 teaspoon dried thyme
salt and pepper

place the diced pork into a deep saucepan and cook slowly until fat melts

add the onion and potatoes and simmer for 15 minutes and then add the tomatoes

add the chopped clams, season with thyme, salt, and pepper, and simmer for 3 minutes

some New Yorkers add chopped green pepper or chopped celery to the ingredients above

(4 servings)

NEW ENGLAND CLAM CHOWDER

1/4 pound salt pork, diced
1 onion, chopped
1 cup cubed potatoes
1 pint chowder clams, finely chopped (or canned clams)
1/2 teaspoon salt
dash pepper
2 cups milk
minced parsley

place the salt pork into a deep saucepan and cook slowly until fat melts

add the onion and potato and simmer for 15 minutes

add the clams and seasoning

add the milk and heat. serve garnished with parsley

(4 servings)

CHARLESTON FISH CHOWDER

2 pounds fish fillets
(almost any kind)
1/4 pound salt pork, diced
2 large onions, diced
few grains cayenne pepper
1/2 teaspoon nutmeg or
allspice
1 teaspoon salt
6 pilot biscuits (more if
desired), broken into
pieces
2 tablespoons catsup
1 cup sherry

sauté the pork, add the onions, and cook until golden

put the fish fillets into a large pot, cover with water, add the salt pork, onions, and the seasonings

thicken with pilot biscuits, cover and cook almost an hour

add the catsup and wine, stir and serve

(4 servings)

BOSTON CLAM CHOWDER

2 dozen chowder clams,
scrubbed
1 quart water
1 stalk celery, diced
1 onion, diced
1 clove garlic, minced
1/2 bay leaf
1 sprig parsley
1/2 cup potatoes, peeled
and diced
1 ounce salt pork, diced
1/2 onion, minced
1/2 stalk celery, finely
chopped
1/2 leek (white part only),
finely chopped
1 tablespoon flour
1/2 cup light cream,
warmed
1 tablespoon butter
minced parsley

put the clams into a large pot with a quart of cold water. add the celery, onion, garlic, bay leaf, and parsley. cover the pot and simmer for 10 minutes

remove the clams (discarding the shells), mince them, and set aside

remove the stock, strain thoroughly and return to the pot. add the potatoes and simmer for 15 minutes or until potatoes are tender

meanwhile, in a second pot, render the pork, add the onion, celery, and leek, and sprinkle with flour. cook for 5 minutes longer, then stir in the hot stock and simmer for 10 minutes

stir in the minced clams, cream, and butter

serve garnished with minced parsley

(4 servings)

NEW ENGLAND FISH CHOWDER

1/4 pound salt pork, diced 2 onions, diced 2 cups hot water 3 potatoes, peeled and diced 3 stalks celery, chopped 1 bay leaf 1 teaspoon salt 1/4 teaspoon pepper 2 pounds cod or haddock fillets, cut into 1-inch cubes 4 cups hot milk 2 tablespoons butter chopped parsley	put the salt pork into a large pot and sauté 1 minute. add the onions and cook until golden add water, potatoes, celery, bay leaf, salt, and pepper. cover and cook 10 minutes, then add the cubed fish simmer 10 minutes or until fish flakes with a fork add the hot milk, stir, check seasoning, and serve garnished with bits of butter and chopped parsley (4 to 6 servings)

LOBSTER (OR SHRIMP) CHOWDER

1/4 pound salt pork, diced 2 tablespoons flour pinch mace pinch cayenne 1 teaspoon salt 3 cups milk 1 cup cream 2 tablespoons butter 1 pound fresh or frozen lobster meat, cut up, or 1 pound fresh shrimp, cup up paprika	in a large saucepan sauté the salt pork, blend in the flour, mace, cayenne, and salt. cook a minute or so stir in the milk, cream, and butter. simmer and stir until thickened and smooth add the lobster meat or shrimp, simmer slowly for 10 minutes, and serve garnished with paprika (4 servings)

MAINE SCROD CHOWDER

1 whole scrod (about
2 pounds), cleaned
2 cups water
1/4 pound salt pork, diced
2 large onions, diced
2 large potatoes, diced
2 cups milk, heated
2 cups cream, heated
salt and pepper
chopped parsley

put the scrod, whole, into a large pot, cover with water and simmer 15 minutes or until fish flakes with a fork. remove fish from the stock and set aside to cool

sauté the pork, add the onions, cook until golden, and add to the stock. add the potatoes and simmer 15 minutes or until potatoes are cooked

meanwhile, remove and discard the skin and bones from the scrod, flake the fish with a fork and add to the stock

heat the milk and cream (do not boil) and add to the chowder. serve garnished with parsley

(4 servings)

RHODE ISLAND OYSTER CHOWDER

2 tablespoons chopped
onion
2 tablespoons butter
1/2 cup water
1/2 cup chopped celery
1 cup potatoes, diced
1 teaspoon salt
1/2 teaspoon pepper
1 pint milk
1 dozen oysters with their
liquor
minced parsley

sauté onion in butter until golden, add water, celery, potatoes, salt, and pepper

cover and cook until vegetables are tender

add milk and heat to just below boiling, then add the oysters and liquor

simmer gently until oysters begin to curl at the edges and serve sprinkled with minced parsley

(2 servings)

BISQUES

OYSTER (OR CLAM) BISQUE

1 stalk celery, chopped
1 slice onion, chopped
1 sprig parsley, chopped
1 bay leaf
1 pint milk
1/4 pound butter
1/4 cup flour
1 dozen oysters or cherrystone clams (with liquor), chopped
1 teaspoon salt
dash pepper

put the celery, onion, parsley, bay leaf, and milk into a saucepan, bring almost to a boil, and simmer for 10 minutes. strain

in the top of a double boiler melt the butter, then add the milk. cook, stirring until thickened and smooth

add the chopped oysters or clams and seasonings. simmer a few minutes and serve

(4 servings)

QUICK CLAM AND TOMATO BISQUE

1 tablespoon butter
1/2 cup chopped celery
1 sprig parsley
1/2 bay leaf
1 slice onion, chopped
pinch nutmeg
1 cup clam broth
1 cup tomato soup
1 cup heavy cream
salt and pepper

sauté the celery, parsley, bay leaf, onion, and nutmeg in the butter for 2 minutes

add the clam broth, tomato soup, and cream. heat but do not boil

put through a sieve, reheat, and season to taste

(4 servings)

CRAWFISH BISQUE

this is a way-out dish from old New Orleans, popular in the days when servants were plentiful and cheap and had nothing to do but sit around all day singing and stuffing crawfish heads. if you have time on your hands—and patience—and if you can get hold of 4 dozen fresh crawfish, this could be fun

4 dozen fresh crawfish, soaked in salt water and well scrubbed
2 quarts hot water
1 cup bread
1 tablespoon butter
1 tablespoon flour
1 onion, finely chopped
1 teaspoon chopped parsley
salt and pepper
1 egg
flour
butter

SAUCE:

3 tablespoons flour
2 tablespoons butter
1 carrot, chopped
1/2 cup chopped celery
1 teaspoon chopped parsley
salt and pepper

boil the crawfish in 2 quarts water for 1/2 hour. pour off the broth and set aside for the sauce

pick the crawfish, clean the heads and save them and the meat from the bodies

soak the bread in water and squeeze it dry. chop the meat and add it to the bread

melt the butter, blend in the flour, add the onion, parsley, salt, and pepper. cook gently a minute or two, then add the crawfish and bread. cook a minute or two longer and transfer to a bowl

add 1 egg, mix well, and stuff into the crawfish heads

sprinkle the heads lightly with flour and fry a few minutes in butter and serve with sauce made by adding a browned butter-flour mixture to the crawfish broth seasoned with carrot, celery, parsley, salt, and pepper

(6 servings)

CRAB BISQUE À LA RECTOR

3 tablespoons butter
3 tablespoons flour
4 cups milk
1/2 teaspoon salt
dash pepper
dash nutmeg
1 tablespoon Worcester-
shire sauce
1/2 pound crabmeat
(fresh or canned)
3 tablespoons sherry wine
1/2 cup unsweetened
whipped cream
paprika

melt the butter, blend in the flour. add the milk gradually, stirring until smooth

add seasonings and simmer 2 minutes

add crabmeat, heat, and stir

stir in the sherry and serve in cups topped with whipped cream and a little paprika

(4 to 6 servings)

LOBSTER BISQUE

1/4 cup olive oil
1/2 pound lobster meat
1 stalk celery, diced
1/2 onion, chopped
1 clove garlic, crushed
1/2 cup flour
1 teaspoon paprika
1 tablespoon tomato puree
salt and pepper
1 quart hot fish stock
(see index)
4 tablespoons butter
1 cup cream

heat the oil in a large pot and add the lobster meat, celery, onion, and garlic. cook, stirring until vegetables are light brown

stir in 1/2 cup flour and add paprika, tomato puree, salt, and pepper

gradually stir in the hot fish stock, reduce the heat, cover, and cook slowly for an hour

put the soup through a sieve, dice the lobster meat, and return it to the soup

heat, add the butter and cream, and serve

(6 servings)

SEAFOOD BISQUE

1 cup tomato juice
1/2 cup tomato puree
1 cup canned shrimp,
      finely chopped
1 cup crabmeat
1 small clove garlic,
      crushed
salt and pepper
1 cup light cream
little lemon juice
paprika
chopped chives, dill, or
      parsley

into a large pot put the tomato juice, tomato puree, shrimp, crabmeat, garlic, salt, and pepper. simmer slowly for 2 minutes

gradually stir in the cream, add a few drops lemon juice, and serve garnished with paprika and chives, dill, or parsley

also good served cold

(4 servings)

SHRIMP BISQUE

4 tablespoons butter
1 stalk celery, chopped
2 large mushrooms,
      chopped
1/2 onion, chopped
1/2 carrot, chopped
pinch marjoram
few grains mace
1/2 teaspoon freshly
      ground pepper
1/2 teaspoon salt
1 can chicken broth
1 cup cooked or canned
shrimp, finely chopped
1 cup heavy cream
2 teaspoons dry sherry

put the butter, celery, mushrooms, onion, carrot, and seasonings into a large pot and sauté slowly for 10 minutes

add the chicken broth and cook 5 minutes longer. put through a sieve

add the chopped shrimp, simmer a minute or so, check the seasoning, and stir in the cream and sherry

serve at once

(6 servings)

BOUILLABAISSE

Bouillabaisse is a great big one-dish fish meal consisting of an ever-varying assortment of seafood—usually shellfish, mollusks and fish—cooked together with wine, water, or fish stock and seasoned with garlic, saffron, and whatever else you can find in the kitchen. The original and perfect bouillabaisse can be made only on the shores of the Mediterranean, or so say the Marseillaise, because several of the necessary fishes cannot be found elsewhere —rascasse and wrasse, for example. But sea robin (usually thrown away in this country), skate, mullet, whiting, and cod serve as able substitutes, so there is no reason to be bashful or self-conscious about cooking up a bouillabaisse wherever you are.

BOUILLABAISSE #1

1/2 cup olive oil
1 carrot, chopped
3 onions, chopped
2 leeks (white parts only), chopped
2 cloves garlic, crushed
1 bay leaf
2 or 3 pounds several kinds of firm fish (cod, mullet, eel, whiting, etc.), cleaned, scaled, boned, and cut into 2-inch chunks
3 tomatoes, peeled and quartered
2 cups fish stock (see index) or clam broth
1 cup cooked or canned shellfish (shrimp, crab, or lobster)
1 dozen mollusks in the shell (oysters, clams, or mussels)
few grains saffron
1 cup dry white wine
salt and pepper

take a large pot. put into it the olive oil, carrot, onions, leeks, garlic, and bay leaf. cook slowly until tender and golden add the fish, tomatoes, and stock. cook 20 minutes longer add the shellfish, mollusks, and saffron and cook until shells open

add the wine, season to taste and serve with hunks of French bread to mop up the sauce

(8 servings)

BOUILLABAISSE #2

2 cups cooked lobster
meat, cut into pieces
3 pounds assorted fish
(red snapper, sea bass,
cod, haddock, etc.),
cleaned, boned, and cut
into pieces
1/2 cup olive oil
2 cloves garlic, crushed
1 bay leaf
1/2 teaspoon thyme
2 tablespoons chopped
parsley
fish stock (see index)
1/2 cup dry white wine
1/2 pound squid, cleaned
(see index) and cut into
slices
1/2 cup chopped tomato
few grains saffron,
powdered
salt and pepper

put the fish pieces, oil, garlic, bay leaf, thyme, and parsley into a large pot and cook, stirring, over low heat for 5 minutes

add enough fish stock to cover, and cook 5 minutes longer

add the wine, squid, tomato, saffron, salt, and pepper, and simmer gently for 10 minutes longer

serve with crusty French bread

(6 servings)

BOUILLABAISSE #3

1 pound eel and 2 pounds striped bass (or bluefish), cleaned, boned and cut into 3-inch pieces
3 pounds lobster, split, cleaned, and with claws cracked
1 onion, sliced
2 cloves garlic, sliced
2 leeks (white parts only), sliced
1 bay leaf
2 teaspoons chopped parsley
2 tablespoons olive oil
3 cups dry white wine
salt and pepper
fish stock (see index)
few grains saffron, powdered

put all the ingredients except the stock and saffron into a shallow glass or stainless steel dish and marinate for about 2 hours, stirring from time to time

add enough fish stock to cover the fish, add the saffron, cover and cook at low heat about 15 minutes, or until fish flakes with a fork

serve with chunks of French bread

(8 servings)

Flour seafood only at the last minute or the fish moisture will come through the flour and make it soggy.

fish stews related to Mediterranean bouillabaisse keep popping up all over the world, composed of whatever seafood and seasonings are indigenous to the locality. Here are two good examples:

MARMITE BRETONNE

5 pounds assorted fish
(flounder, red snapper,
eel, sea bass, haddock,
whiting, etc.), cleaned,
boned, and cut into large
chunks
salt and pepper
few grains cayenne
fish fumet (see index)
2 cups heavy cream
4 tablespoons butter

put the fish into a large pot.
season with salt, pepper, and
cayenne, cover with fish fumet, and simmer slowly for 15
minutes

add the cream and butter and
simmer a minute longer

check seasoning and serve in
shallow soup plates, a little of
each fish to a person

(6 servings)

FLORIDA FISH STEW

1 large onion, chopped
2 leeks (white parts only),
chopped
2 cloves garlic, chopped
1/2 cup oil
1 bay leaf
2 tomatoes, peeled and
chopped
2 teaspoons salt
2 teaspoons peppercorns
2 pounds pompano,
cleaned, boned, and cut
into pieces
2 cups lobster meat, cut
into pieces
hot water
1 dozen soft clams,
scrubbed
1/2 cup dry white wine

in a large pot, sauté the onion, leek, and garlic in the oil
until golden

add the bay leaf, tomatoes,
salt, and peppercorns. stir

add the pompano, lobster
meat, and enough hot water to
cover. bring to a boil, cover,
and cook 5 minutes

add the clams and cook 2 minutes longer or until shells open

add the wine, cook another
minute, and serve in soup
plates with Italian bread

(6 servings)

GUMBOS

LOBSTER GUMBO

4 tablespoons butter
1 onion, chopped
1 clove garlic, crushed
1 stalk celery, chopped
1 large tomato, peeled and chopped
2 cups sliced okra, canned or fresh
1 bay leaf
pinch thyme
few dashes Tabasco
salt and pepper
1 quart boiling water
1/2 pound lobster meat, cut into pieces

melt the butter in a large pot and sauté onion, garlic, and celery about 10 minutes or until golden

add the tomato, okra, and seasonings. stir in the boiling water, cover, and simmer for half an hour

add the lobster meat and continue simmering 10 minutes longer

serve with rice

(6 servings)

OYSTER GUMBO FILÉ

2 tablespoons flour
1 tablespoon butter
1 tablespoon oil
1 onion, chopped
1 green pepper, seeded and chopped
pinch thyme
1 bay leaf
few drops Tabasco
salt and pepper
water
2 dozen oysters with their liquor
2 teaspoons chopped parsley
1 tablespoon filé (dried sassafras leaves)

blend the flour, butter, and oil in a large pot, add the vegetables and seasonings. cook slowly for a minute or so

add enough water to the oyster liquor to make about 3 quarts of liquid. add this to the pot, cover, and simmer for half an hour

add the oysters and chopped parsley and cook about 5 minutes, or until the oysters curl at the edges

remove from the stove, drop in the filé, and stir vigorously until thickened

serve with rice

(6 servings)

NEW ORLEANS SHRIMP (OR CRAB) GUMBO

4 slices bacon
2 cups sliced okra
(fresh or canned)
2 tablespoons butter
1 onion, chopped
1 clove garlic, crushed
1 green pepper, chopped
1 stalk celery, chopped
2 tomatoes, skinned and
chopped
pinch thyme
1 quart hot water
salt and pepper
1 pound shelled, raw
shrimp or cooked
crabmeat

fry the bacon to a crisp, break into bits and set aside

add the butter to the bacon fat and then add the okra, onion, garlic, pepper, and celery. sauté for about 10 minutes (canned okra takes less time)

add the tomatoes, thyme, the hot water, salt, and pepper. cover and simmer about 1/2 hour, then toss in the shrimp or crabmeat. simmer 10 minutes longer, check seasoning, and serve garnished with the bacon bits

(6 servings)

Don't fry seafood in butter alone. Before the heat is high enough to cook the seafood, the butter will burn. Mix the butter half-and-half with oil.

FISH AND SHELLFISH ENTREES

The fishes of the sea, and of the lakes and ponds, and rivers and streams differ each from the other in a great many ways. In fact, it sometimes seems that the only thing they have in common is that they all live in water. Fish may be covered with large or small scales, or they may have none. They may have big bulging eyes, tiny eyes, or no eyes at all. Or, both eyes may grow on the same side of the body—the right side or the left. Some fish have "legs," some seem to have "wings."

The flesh itself can be red, white, blue, or black. It can be tender and flaky, or firm and tough, coarse or fine, fat or lean.

Differences in shape and in size are also clearly apparent. Fish can be flat or thick, long and skinny, or round and chubby. And, they can weigh half a ton or a fraction of an ounce. Shellfish, too, have their similarities and differences. Lobsters come with or without claws, crabs vary all the way from the king crab of Alaska, valuable for their legs, to the stone crab of Florida of which only the claws are eaten. Clams and cockles are alike—but different, squid and octopus are alike—but different, and so are terrapin and turtles.

All these peculiarities or characteristics call for consideration when it comes to preparing seafood for the dinner table. Lean fish, such as red snapper, cod, flounder, swordfish, etc., usually require brushing with oil or basting with a fumet as they are baked or broiled, and are frequently served with a sauce. Fat fish—mackerel, bluefish, tuna, trout, etc.—cook successfully in their own fatty juices and may be served as is, garnished with a little butter and a wedge of lemon.

It goes without saying that the same recipe in a great many cases may be followed for cooking fish of similar fat content, providing, of course, that there is a similarity also in size.

ABALONE

Oysters, clams, scallops, and mussels, you may have noticed, all have two shells—one on the north (or top) side and one on the south (or bottom) side. But shed a tear for the poor abalone who, alas, has but one shell. This he uses as a sort of umbrella covering his large muscular foot with which he attaches himself to rocks. The shell is large, running 6 to 8 inches in diameter, and the meat is tough. If you live in Topeka, Sioux City, Knoxville, or Bismarck, the toughness of the abalone muscle won't much bother you, but coastal Californians are very much concerned because the flavor is so delectable that abalone eaters can't keep away from them and spend a great deal of their lives pounding the hell out of little 3/8-inch-thick steaks to render them chewable.

Canned abalone is generally available, and I understand that it is sometimes possible to find abalone steaks in a frozen state. If you are lucky enough to find them, you will probably be spared the usual tenderizing exercise since the frozen steaks have been prepounded.

FRIED ABALONE

2 pounds abalone, cleaned, sliced, and well pounded
salt and pepper
2 eggs, beaten
1 cup fine, dry bread crumbs, or cracker meal
1/2 cup olive oil

wipe the abalone slices dry, sprinkle with salt and pepper, dip into beaten egg and then into bread crumbs

heat the oil in a heavy skillet and brown the abalone 1 1/2 minutes on each side

serve immediately

(6 servings)

ABALONE IN CASSEROLE

2 pounds abalone, fried (see previous recipe)
1 onion, chopped
1 clove garlic, crushed
1 tablespoon tomato puree
1 teaspoon prepared mustard
1/2 cup chopped parsley
1 tablespoon lemon juice
1 cup water

remove abalone from skillet to a casserole

in the skillet, sauté the onion and garlic, taking care not to burn them

add the tomato puree, mustard, parsley, lemon juice, and water

simmer for about 5 minutes and pour into casserole with the abalone

place casserole into preheated 350° oven and bake for 1 hour

(6 servings)

PAN BROILED ABALONE STEAKS

2 pounds abalone,
cleaned and pounded
into 1/2-inch steaks
juice of 2 lemons
1 teaspoon paprika
1/2 teaspoon salt
1 teaspoon chopped
parsley
2 teaspoons butter
bearnaise sauce (see
index)

marinate the steaks in the seasoned lemon juice for an hour

broil in a heavy, hot skillet for 5 minutes on each side, or until golden

garnish with butter and chopped parsley and serve with bearnaise sauce

(4 servings)

ABALONE STEAKS AU BEURRE NOIR

2 pounds abalone steaks
1 teaspoon salt
1/2 teaspoon white pepper
1 egg, beaten
dry bread crumbs
1 tablespoon bacon fat (or
olive oil)
beurre noir (see index)

if the steaks have not been tenderized, pound them gently until all the fibers have been relaxed

season the steaks with salt and pepper, dip first in egg, then in bread crumbs, and sauté in bacon fat over moderate heat for about 5 minutes or until slightly browned and tender to the fork. (care must be taken to pound well, to keep the heat low, and not to cook too long)

serve with *beurre noir*

(4 servings)

BASS

B-A-S-S—a four-letter word covering a multitude of fins (sorry), ranging all the way from the small calico bass found in streams and lakes all over the world to the enormous black sea bass (weighing up to 600 pounds) found off the California coast. Sometimes there seems no limit to the variety of fish included in this species: sunfish, blue gills, crappie, small and large-mouth bass, spotted and redeye bass of fresh-water streams and lakes; sea bass, black sea bass, white sea bass, striped bass, and rock fish are a few of the better known bass from the sea.

In general, the bass is a thick-bodied, firm-fleshed, lean fish with pronounced spines and large scales. Small varieties may be scaled, eviscerated, and pan-fried in a little butter. The larger varieties may be split and broiled or broiled as steaks. Try baking them in a hot oven, with or without one of the stuffings discussed later (see index).

FRESH-WATER BASS, CAMP STYLE

2 pounds small-mouth, large-mouth or calico bass, or sunfish, blue gill, or crappie, dressed
2 teaspoons salt
pepper
1/2 cup cornmeal, yellow or white
1/2 cup flour
2 tablespoons butter
2 tablespoons bacon fat
2 teaspoons chopped parsley
1 lemon, sliced

dress the fish (see index), wipe them dry with a paper towel and season well with salt and pepper

roll them in a mixture of cornmeal and flour until well coated

heat the butter and bacon fat in a skillet and brown the fish for 4 minutes on each side, or until golden brown, and flesh flakes when fork-tested

serve at once, garnished with chopped parsley and lemon slices

(4 to 6 servings)

the above recipe will serve well for almost any small freshwater pan fry such as brook trout, perch, pickerel, etc. . . . and you can use bread crumbs or cracker meal in place of cornmeal, and almost any kind of fat or vegetable oil

BROILED STRIPED BASS MAÎTRE D'HÔTEL

3 pounds striped bass, cleaned, and split
1 teaspoon salt
1/2 teaspoon pepper
1/2 cup maître d'hôtel sauce (see index)
1 teaspoon chopped tarragon
1 lemon, quartered

wipe the fish dry, season with salt and pepper, and cook according to broiling directions
serve on a hot platter, spread generously with maître d'hôtel sauce, and garnish with chopped fresh tarragon and lemon wedges
(4 servings)

bluefish, spanish mackerel, shad, rockfish, and lake trout all lend themselves nicely to this same treatment

STRIPED BASS WITH MUSHROOM STUFFING

1 striped bass (about 4 pounds), dressed and boned
1 teaspoon salt
mushroom stuffing (see index)
2 tablespoons melted butter
4 slices bacon
chopped parsley
1 lemon, sliced

wipe fish dry and season inside and out with salt
stuff fish loosely with mushroom stuffing, close with skewers, and brush with melted butter
place fish into a greased baking pan, cover with bacon slices, and bake in a preheated 375° oven for 40 minutes or until flesh flakes when tested
serve garnished with chopped parsley and lemon slices
(6 servings)

or try one of the other stuffings described later in this chapter (see index)

striped bass

BLACK SEA BASS WITH OLIVE SAUCE

3 pounds black sea bass
steak (or steaks)
1 teaspoon salt
1/4 cup butter
1 clove garlic, crushed
1/4 cup sliced olives
(ripe, green, or stuffed)
1 teaspoon paprika
1/2 teaspoon pepper
2 teaspoons lemon juice
chopped fresh dill

salt the steak and pan broil it in a heavy skillet, using a little oil if necessary to prevent sticking (test with a fork and remove when fish is flaky—3 minutes on each side should do it). set aside on a warm platter

using the same skillet, melt the butter, add the garlic, olives, paprika, pepper, and lemon juice and sauté gently for a few minutes

pour the sauce over the steak and garnish with chopped fresh dill

(4 servings)

alternate steaks: king mackerel, grouper, tuna

BLOWFISH

This is the Cinderella fish that nobody wanted. You go fishing in any shallow water along the Atlantic Coast and no matter what you're after, you get blowfish. These ugly little animals inflate themselves on being caught to fool you into throwing them back, but if you know a thing or two, you'll keep them, because along the spine there is hidden a most delicious, tender morsel of white, boneless meat. The trick is to get at it, since the blowfish is armored with an almost impenetrable, tough, sandpaper-like skin. I use an axe, chop off the head, turn them inside out, and then chop off the tail. (A good fish knife will do the trick, too.) The morsel you have left is sold in fish markets all along the East Coast as sea squab. It's recommended!

GOLDEN BROWN BLOWFISH

8 blowfish, dressed
1 teaspoon salt
1/2 teaspoon pepper
1/2 cup flour
1/2 cup finely ground
white cornmeal
1 cup cooking oil
parsley sprigs
1 lemon, sliced

pat the blowfish dry with a paper towel, season with salt and pepper

blend the flour and cornmeal and roll the blowfish in the mixture until well covered

heat the oil (but do not let it smoke) and fry the blowfish one or two at a time for 2 minutes on each side or until golden

serve garnished with parsley sprigs and lemon slices

(4 servings)

vary the above delicious dish by serving the blowfish with sauce ravigote, sauce normandie, or maître d'hôtel (see index)

BLUEFISH

This big beautiful fish is a culinary favorite all up and down the Atlantic Coast. Although they run, on the average, about 10 pounds, bluefish found in the market range between 1 and 6 pounds. Usually they are sold whole.

SHRIMP-STUFFED BLUEFISH

1/4 pound butter
1/4 cup finely chopped shallots or scallions
1/2 cup flour
2 cups fish stock (see index)
1 pound shrimp, cooked, peeled, and finely chopped
1/2 cup finely chopped mushrooms
1/2 teaspoon salt
few grains cayenne
1 three pound bluefish, dressed and split with backbone removed
parsley

sauté the shallots in the butter over low heat. do not brown. stir in the flour and then the fish stock, simmer about 5 minutes and add the shrimp, mushrooms, salt, and cayenne. continue to cook until thickened

place this stuffing onto one half of the fish and cover with the other half, reserving a little to use as a sauce

place in a buttered ovenproof dish and bake, uncovered, in a preheated 400° oven about half an hour, or until flesh flakes when fork-tested

place on a heated platter, spoon on the remaining stuffing, and garnish with parsley sprigs

(4 servings)

if a lean fish is substituted (pollock, red snapper, haddock, cod, etc.) fish should be brushed generously with oil before baking

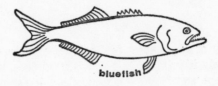

bluefish

BLUEFISH WITH CAPER STUFFING

1 bluefish (about 4 pounds), dressed
1 teaspoon salt
1/4 teaspoon pepper
caper stuffing (see index)
2 tablespoons melted butter
1/2 cup fish stock
1 onion, sliced
paprika
1 lemon, sliced

wipe fish dry and season inside and out with salt and pepper

stuff fish loosely and brush with melted butter

place fish into baking pan with the fish stock, cover with onion slices, and bake in a preheated 400° oven for half an hour or until flesh flakes when fork-tested

serve garnished with paprika and lemon slices

(6 servings)

SAUTÉED BUTTERFISH

4 pounds butterfish (about 1/2 pound each), eviscerated, but with heads and tails intact
1 teaspoon salt
1/2 teaspoon pepper
1/2 cup cornmeal
1/2 cup flour
2 tablespoons butter
2 tablespoons cooking oil
chopped watercress
1 lemon, quartered

wipe the fish dry, season with salt and pepper, and roll in a mixture of flour and cornmeal

heat the butter and oil (do not allow to smoke), and fry the fish about 3 minutes on each side or until golden

serve garnished with chopped watercress and lemon wedges

(4 servings)

CARP

Carp, a family of fresh water fish, originally indigenous to Asia, has been widely introduced into the lakes, ponds, streams, and rivers of Europe and North America where it has multiplied almost unbelievably. The carp likes to live in muddy, sluggish water where he doesn't have to go in for strenuous exercise fighting

70 the complete seafood cookbook

currents. As a result, the meat, while firm and white, often has a muddy flavor, especially when taken from warmish waters.

Carp is especially valued by Jews who use it in many recipes. They make certain it is fresh by purchasing it alive and taking it home in a pail of water. In Israel, you're nobody if you don't have a carp pool in your back yard!

In the American market, carp is found in sizes ranging from 2 to 8 pounds, and is often sold live from tanks.

Members of the large carp family include bream, chub (whitefish), dace, goldfish, gudgeon, minnow, and roach (not the insect).

SAUTÉED CARP WITH SAUTERNE

1 dressed carp (3 to 5 pounds)
1/2 cup vinegar diluted with 2 cups water
1/2 cup butter
1/2 cup olive (or peanut) oil
1 teaspoon salt
1/4 teaspoon pepper
flour
1 cup dry sauterne or other dry white wine
1 tablespoon prepared horseradish
1 egg yolk, lightly beaten
1 tablespoon chopped chives

wash the carp in the diluted vinegar to kill whatever muddy flavor it might have, then pat it dry with a paper towel

heat the butter and oil in a heavy skillet. season the carp with salt and pepper, dust it lightly with flour, and place it in the skillet

pour the wine over the fish, cover, and sauté gently for half an hour or until fish flakes when fork-tested, baste occasionally

remove fish to a serving platter and keep hot

stir the horseradish into the skillet liquid. add a little of the liquid to the egg yolk, then stir it into the sauce. pour over the fish, garnish with chopped chives, and serve at once

(4 to 6 servings)

CARP IN BURGUNDY

1 dressed carp (3 to 5
    pounds)
2 onions, chopped
1/2 cup fish fumet (see
    index)
1 cup burgundy wine
4 anchovy fillets
2 teaspoons flour
    creamed with
2 teaspoons butter
1 egg yolk, lightly beaten

place the onions and then the fish into a greased, foil-lined baking dish, add the fumet, burgundy, and garnish with anchovy fillets

bake, uncovered, in a pre-heated 350° oven about half an hour or until fish flakes easily, basting often with the pan liquid

remove the fish to a preheated platter and strain the liquid

place the liquid into a small saucepan, heat, stir in the flour creamed with the butter, and simmer for a minute

add a little of the hot liquid to the egg yolk, then stir it into the sauce. pour over the fish and serve at once

(4 to 6 servings)

How to tell a good wine before you open the bottle: get a wine merchant you can trust.

carp

CATFISH

Catfish, usually associated with the Mississippi River and its tributaries, show up all over the world. They come in all sizes, ranging from less than a pound to more than 100 pounds. (I recently saw a photograph of a catfish taken from the Mekong River in Vietnam weighing 300 pounds!)

In the raw, the catfish is an ugly, smooth-skinned creature with long barbels resembling cat's whiskers, but the meat is sweet, firm, flaky, and flavorful, and is prized as a delicacy all over the world. It has been estimated that in this country alone more than 10 tons of catfish are eaten every year—and that's a lot of catfish!

The Department of Interior has set up a number of fish farms in the United States for the express purpose of cultivating this prolific and nutritious fish. Originally concentrated in the state of Arkansas, catfish farms, inexpensive to start and profitable to run, are beginning to show up all over the midwest.

CURRIED CATFISH

3 pounds catfish, skinned, cleaned, and decapitated

3 cups water

2 onions, chopped

3 tablespoons chopped parsley

1 teaspoon salt

1/2 teaspoon pepper

1 tablespoon butter

1 tablespoon flour

2 teaspoons curry powder

cut the catfish into pieces 4 inches long, put them into a stewpot with the water, onions, parsley, salt, and pepper

cook for 15 minutes or until flesh flakes when fork-tested

remove the fish to a heated serving platter and keep hot

cook liquid uncovered, until it is reduced to about 1 cup

combine the butter, flour, and curry powder, add to it the cooking liquid, cook, and stir until sauce is thickened

check seasoning, pour over the fish, and serve hot

(4 servings)

SOUR CATFISH

3 pounds catfish, skinned, cleaned, and decapitated
3 cups water
4 bay leaves
3 cloves
10 allspice
10 whole peppercorns
1 onion, chopped
1 teaspoon sugar
1 1/2 cups vinegar
2 teaspoons salt

put the catfish head (or heads) into a stewpot with the remaining ingredients and boil for 10 minutes

remove the head and discard

cut the catfish into 4-inch pieces, add them to the pot, and stew for 15 minutes or until flesh flakes when fork-tested

remove the fish to a serving dish, pour the sauce over it, and set aside

when cold it is like jelly and ready to serve

(4 servings)

CATFISH WITH SHRIMP SAUCE

2 1/2 pounds catfish (fillet or steak)
1/2 teaspoon salt
dash white pepper
1 cup milk
1 cup white cornmeal (waterground, preferably)
1/4 cup cooking oil
1/4 cup butter
shrimp sauce (see index)

season the catfish with salt and pepper, dip in milk, then in cornmeal. sauté in butter and oil about 5 minutes on each side or until golden

remove to hot serving platter and serve with shrimp sauce

(4 servings)

catfish

CATFISH AU BEURRE NOIR

3 pounds catfish,
dressed and split
1 cup butter
2 tablespoons flour
2 teaspoons chopped
fresh mint
2 teaspoons salt
1/4 teaspoon pepper
4 tablespoons chopped
parsley
1 lemon, sliced

melt the butter in a saucepan and use part of it to brush fish on all sides

dust fish lightly with flour and place on greased broiling pan. sprinkle with mint, salt, and pepper, place 2 inches below broiler and cook about 8 minutes or until fish flakes when fork-tested. brush occasionally with melted butter. remove to heated platter

meanwhile add the parsley to the butter and cook over low heat until butter is brown. pour sauce over the fish, serve garnished with lemon slices

(4 servings)

When using flour, don't season the flour; season the fish.

A 200° oven will keep food warm without cooking.

CATFISH EN PAPILLOTE

4 catfish steaks
(about 2 pounds)
court-bouillon #2
(made with white wine)
2 tablespoons butter
2 tablespoons chopped
shallots
1 cup sliced mushrooms
2 tablespoons flour
1/2 teaspoon salt
few grains cayenne
2 tablespoons cream

poach the steaks gently in the court-bouillon for 6 minutes. remove from the skillet and set aside

strain the poaching liquid, reduce to 1 cup at high heat, and set aside

sauté the shallots and mushrooms in butter at low heat for 2 or 3 minutes—do not brown. stir in the flour, salt, and cayenne, and cook another minute

add the reduced poaching liquid and stir-cook until smooth and thick. add the cream and taste for seasoning

cut parchment cooking paper into 4-12-inch ovals, brush with butter, fold vertically, then open again

place a fish steak onto the right half of each papillote, spoon on some of the sauce, fold the left half over, and seal the edges by crimping them together

place the papillotes onto a greased cookie sheet and bake in a preheated 450° oven for about 8 minutes

serve in the parchment which will be puffed up and brown

(4 servings)

aluminum foil can be used in place of parchment, but it must be well buttered or the steaks are apt to take on a metallic flavor

CATFISH CREOLE

2-1/2 pounds sliced catfish
4 tablespoons butter
salt
freshly ground pepper
4 slices peeled tomato
1/2 green pepper, chopped
1 medium onion, chopped
2 tablespoons chopped
fresh dill

place the catfish slices into a well buttered baking pan, season with salt and pepper, and add the tomato slices, green pepper, and onion

bake for half an hour in a preheated 350° oven, basting occasionally. serve garnished with chopped dill

(4 servings)

alternate steaks: cod, pollock

CATFISH STEAKS WITH MINT

4 catfish steaks
(about 2-1/2 pounds)
4 tablespoons oil
1 teaspoon salt
white pepper
2 teaspoons chopped
fresh mint
1 tablespoon chopped
parsley
1 clove garlic, chopped
1-1/2 cups dry bread
crumbs
4 slices lemon

wipe the steaks dry, brush both sides with oil, and season with salt and pepper

mix the mint, parsley, garlic, and bread crumbs

roll the steaks in the crumb mixture and pour the remaining oil over each

place in a broiler rack and broil about 4 inches below the heat for about 6 minutes on each side

serve with lemon slices

(4 servings)

alternate steaks: cod, pollock

CISCO

Cisco, or lake herring, is one of the prized fish of the Great Lakes. The fully grown fish sometimes reaches 2 pounds. Cook it as you would herring.

CLAMS

There are many types of clams lying around in the shallow waters of the world, but two species lead the field: the quahogs, or hard clams (called chowders, cherrystones, or little necks, depending upon size) and the manninose, or soft clams.

Hard clams are in plentiful supply all up and down the Atlantic Coast of the United States and to some slight extent on the Pacific Coast. They are taken commercially by dredging and raking, but the fun way to get yourself a mess of clams is to go toeing for them. You wade around in shallow, sandy water, wiggling your toes until they make contact. On a good day and in a good spot, you can fill a basket in no time.

Soft clams, found almost anywhere there is sand on both sides of the Atlantic, bury themselves but maintain contact with the world by the neck-like siphons (these, of course, give away their hiding place during low tide).

The variety of clams is almost endless. California is famous for pismo clams—even named a beach for them—Washington state boasts a razor clam, and New England a beach or surf clam. There is a jackknife clam, a round clam, a horse clam, a mud clam, and a sea clam—all related, but each different in some way. And, they're all edible, but some, like razor clams, are unable to close up tight enough to retain their vital juices, and therefore never get to the market.

One hot August evening at sundown, I watched a crane unload giant gunnysacks of clams from a fishing boat. The clams, measuring a full six inches across, had been dredged from the sea shelf off the New Jersey coast. And there must have been 500 sacks full; they were on their way to a nearby cannery. With so many clams dredged by one small boat in one day, it is difficult to imagine the enormity of the catch along the Atlantic in a year's time.

And then there are cockles, kissing-cousins of clams—sold in "Dublin's fair city" to the cry of "mussels and cockles, alive, alive-o!" and "grown" by contrary Mistress Mary in her garden— and gathered and sold, not only in Ireland, but also up and down the Pacific Coast of the United States and along the South Atlantic and Gulf coasts. Cockles, like clams, come in all sizes, but they differ in appearance, having radial ridges similar to the scallop. When viewed in profile, cockles are heart-shaped. Although you'll find those who disagree, the general opinion is that cockles are less delicate in flavor than clams.

Like oysters, clams—and cockles, too—may be steamed, stewed, scalloped, or fried, broiled, baked, or creamed. In fact, most of the recipes given for oysters may be followed for clams.

STEAMED CLAMS

3 dozen soft-shell clams, well scrubbed
1/2 cup water
2 stalks celery with leaves
1/4 pound butter, melted

put water and celery into a large pot and bring to a boil

put clams into a large sieve or collander and insert into the pot. cover and steam for about 6 minutes or until clams open

serve clams in soup plates with dishes of melted butter on the side

strain the broth and serve in bouillon cups

(2 servings)

(for 4 servings, go through the process again and everyone will have hot clams)

CLAMBAKE, NEW ENGLAND STYLE

no seafood cookbook can be called complete without including the New England clambake. And here's how you do one:
1. dig a large hole in the sand and line it with rocks
2. build a fine, hot fire and lay on more large rocks
3. when the rocks are good and hot, and the fire has died out, cover with a layer of seaweed
4. add 6 live lobsters and another layer of seaweed
5. now, add 6 or 8 dozen cherrystone clams (or steamers) and a thick layer of seaweed
6. cover with a canvas tarpaulin, weighted down with rocks
bake for about 20 minutes or until clams begin to open
serve with plenty of beer

(6 servings)

CLAMBAKE, LANDLUBBER STYLE

1. cover the bottom of a washboiler or large enamel pot with clean seaweed. add a quart of water and place over high heat
2. when water boils add 2 chickens, quartered, each part wrapped in cheesecloth and a layer of seaweed. cover
3. fifteen minutes later add 4 1-1/2 pound lobsters, and another layer of seaweed. cover
4. seven minutes later add 8 ears of corn, husked and each ear wrapped in foil, and another layer of seaweed. cover
5. ten minutes later add 6 dozen steamer clams. cover and steam until clams open

cut the lobsters in half lengthwise and serve the whole mess with melted butter and the kettle liquid as a dip

(8 servings)

White pepper is considered more delicate in flavor than black and therefore more suitable for seasoning seafood.

soft clam

razor clam

quahog clam

COD AND HADDOCK

These two important food fishes run together in the cold waters of the Atlantic and Pacific. Cod, the larger of the two, averages from 10 to 12 pounds near the coast, but reach 25 pounds off the Grand Banks of Newfoundland and have been known to reach well over 200 pounds.

Both cod and haddock are abundant from Newfoundland to Scotland. In the spring and fall when the fish come up to the shallower waters from the ocean depths, the banks and shoals of the North Atlantic are thick with fishing boats from New England, Canada, Iceland, Greenland, Norway, Britain, Portugal, Russia, and Japan.

The meat of these admirable fish is lean, white, and flaky, and is available on the market in almost any form: fresh, frozen, smoked, salted, pickled, and canned; whole, shredded, and filleted; in steaks or in sticks.

The young cod, known as scrod, more delicate in texture and sweeter in flavor, weighing about 2 pounds, are a favorite delicacy in the spring along the Atlantic Coast.

There is no haddock comparable in flavor to the dried and smoked fish originally from the hamlet of Findon, near Aberdeen. This Findon haddock is known to the world as *finnan haddie,* all because the Scots speak English with such a bad accent.

Closely related fish to cod and haddock are hake (also called whiting), and pollock. They are frequently caught in the same nets.

BAKED COD WITH OYSTER STUFFING

1 cod (about 4 pounds), dressed	wipe fish dry and season inside and out with salt and pepper
1 teaspoon salt	stuff fish loosely and brush with Tabasco-butter mixture
1/4 teaspoon pepper	
oyster stuffing (see index)	place fish into a well greased baking pan, cover with bread crumbs and bacon strips, and bake in a preheated 400° oven for half an hour or until flesh flakes when fork-tested
2 tablespoons melted butter mixed with dash Tabasco	
2 tablespoons bread crumbs	
3 strips bacon	serve garnished with lemon slices
1 lemon, sliced	
	(6 servings)

COD STEAKS IN CREAM

4 1/2-pound cod steaks
(or 2 one-pound steaks)
flour (or rice flour)
4 tablespoons butter,
melted
1 cup sliced mushrooms
1/4 cup sliced shallots (or
onions)
1/2 clove garlic, chopped
1/2 cup dry white wine
1 bay leaf
1 cup heavy cream
salt
white pepper
chopped parsley

pat the steaks dry, dust lightly with flour and bake 15 minutes in a preheated 400° oven, basting frequently with melted butter

combine the mushrooms, shallots, garlic, and wine. spoon onto the steaks, add the bay leaf, cover, and cook 15 minutes longer

remove the steaks onto a heated platter, discarding the bay leaf

add the cream to the baking dish, season to taste, and heat until the sauce thickens (do not boil)

season to taste, pour the sauce over the steaks and garnish with chopped parsley
(4 servings)

alternate steaks: salmon, swordfish, halibut, or lingcod

cod

CURRIED CODFISH STEAKS

4 codfish steaks (about 3 pounds)	heat the oil in a heavy skillet and sauté the steaks gently for 2 minutes on each side
1 tablespoon cooking oil	
2 tablespoons lemon juice	combine the lemon juice, melted butter, wine, salt, and pepper, and add it to the skillet
4 tablespoons melted butter	
1/2 cup dry white wine	cook the steaks 5 minutes longer on each side, basting frequently with the sauce
4 scallions, finely chopped	
1/2 teaspoon salt	combine the bread crumbs, cheese, and curry powder, and spread the mixture on the steaks
1/2 teaspoon pepper (preferably white)	
1/2 cup dry bread crumbs	baste again and place the skillet under the broiler for 2 or 3 minutes or until brown
1/2 cup grated cheese	
1 teaspoon curry powder	(4 servings)

alternate steaks: salmon, swordfish, halibut, or lingcod

There are many varieties of peppercorns—each with a subtly different flavor.

CRABS

The crab is probably the most interesting and most versatile of all shellfish. It is the largest of all crustacea and at the same time, the smallest. There are crabs that swim, and those that crawl. Some species are gastronomically valuable only for the legs, others only for the claws or for the body.

The Alaskan King crab, a leggy creature, has no claws and almost no body. He can't even swim. But, he grows to an average of 5 feet across and can average 8 or 10 pounds in weight. The enormous legs are frozen or steamed and shipped to markets all over the world.

The oyster crab moves into the shell of an oyster when still in the larva stage and spends his life there, neither swimming nor moving about, sharing the food pumped in by his host. Pale pink in color, and with a soft shell that never grows hard, this tiny crab never grows larger than your little finger nail, but it has a delicately delicious flavor and is highly prized for use in fish sauces.

There is a stone crab that lives in the sands of Florida and environs measuring only 3 or 4 inches across. The stone crab has disproportionately large claws tinted cream and red and tipped with black. The claws alone are eaten steamed, cracked, and dipped in butter, or cold with a piquant sauce.

The Dungeness crab found along the Pacific Coast from the Aleutian archipelago to Baja California has a large, reddish-brown body measuring up to 10 or 12 inches across and containing a plentiful supply of good, tender meat.

Then there is rock crab, Jonah crab, lady crab, calico crab, green crab, and red crab.

But the most plentiful and perhaps the most prized of all crabs is the blue crab found along the Atlantic Coast from Cape Cod to Florida and in concentrated quantities on the bottom of the Chesapeake and Delaware bays. This scrappy creature measures up to 6 inches across, is dark-green on top, creamy-white beneath, and has large bluish claws.

Crabs are available in the market live or cooked. The meat, sweet, tender, and firm is picked from the shell of the freshly steamed crab, packed, chilled, and sold fresh by the pound in several grades: back fin, lump, flake, and claw meat—in order of cost. Crabmeat also comes canned or frozen.

SOFT-SHELL CRABS are molting crabs that are taken just after shedding their hard shells and before their new shells have hardened. Commercially all soft-shell crabs are blue crabs, since state laws prohibit the marketing of soft-shell Dungeness crabs.

DEVILED CRABS

1 pound crabmeat
1/4 teaspoon English mustard
1/4 teaspoon mace
dash cayenne pepper
1 tablespoon chopped parsley
1 teaspoon Worcestershire sauce
3 tablespoons melted butter
1 tablespoon lemon juice
1 egg, beaten
1/4 cup dry bread crumbs

add the seasonings to the crab-meat, stir in the melted butter, lemon juice, and beaten egg

place into 4 well-buttered shells or ramekins, sprinkle with bread crumbs, and bake in a preheated 350° oven for 15 minutes or until golden

(4 servings)

IMPERIAL CRAB

4 crabs, or 3/4 pound lump or back fin crabmeat and 4 shells
1/2 onion, chopped
2 tablespoons butter
1/2 teaspoon salt
few grains cayenne pepper
dash Worcestershire sauce
1 teaspoon English mustard
2 tablespoons chopped green pepper
2 cups heavy cream
yolks of 2 eggs
dry bread crumbs
butter

boil the crabs, remove the meat, save the shells

sauté the onion in the butter, add the crabmeat, seasonings, green pepper, cream, and mix well

bind with egg yolk, pile into the shells, sprinkle with bread crumbs, dot with butter, and brown in the oven

(4 servings)

CHESAPEAKE BAY CRAB CAKES

**1 pound cooked blue
crabmeat
1/2 teaspoon English
mustard
2 tablespoons mayonnaise
1 egg, beaten
1/2 teaspoon salt
dash cayenne pepper
dry bread crumbs
cooking oil**

combine the crabmeat with the mustard, mayonnaise, egg, salt, and cayenne, shape into 4 cakes and roll in bread crumbs

place the cakes in a heavy frying pan with the oil and cook at moderate heat until brown on one side, then turn and brown the other side

or fry the cakes in deep fat (see index)

(4 servings)

CRAB CIOPPINO

this is a dish you find in the restaurants along the wharves of San Francisco. It's often made with a variety of seafood, but I prefer it with crab alone

**4 large live crabs
1 cup chopped onion
1 cup chopped parsley
1 cup olive oil
2 large cans tomatoes
2 tablespoons tomato paste
2 teaspoons chopped basil
salt
pepper**

kill the crabs by cutting off the face with a sharp knife, remove the shell, the whitish-colored gills, and the spongy digestive organs located in the middle of the body, slice off the top of the inner skeleton, and crack the claws

place crabs into a large kettle and add the onion, parsley, and olive oil. cover, and simmer for 15 to 20 minutes

heat the tomatoes and tomato paste and pour onto the crabs. sprinkle with basil, season with salt and pepper, and cover, cooking for 1/2 hour

serve with chunks of French bread

(4 servings)

CRABMEAT CURRY

1 large onion, finely
chopped
1 clove garlic, finely
chopped
6 tablespoons butter
2 teaspoons curry
powder
3 tablespoons flour
2-1/2 cups cream
dash Tabasco sauce
1-1/2 pounds cooked
crabmeat
salt
4 cups cooked rice
1 cup crisp bacon,
crumbled
2 hard-cooked eggs,
chopped
2 tablespoons chopped
chives

sauté the onions and garlic in butter at low heat for 2 or 3 minutes—do not brown

stir in the curry powder, then the flour, and cook for 2 minutes longer, then gradually add the cream and Tabasco, stirring constantly until smooth and thickened

stir in the crabmeat and season to taste

serve on hot rice topped with bacon bits, chopped egg, and chives

(4 servings)

cooked lobster meat or shrimp may be substituted for crabmeat

STEAMED CRABS

on almost any hot evening on the Eastern Shore of Maryland, if you look closely enough, you are likely to find a crab feast in session. and, if you can get yourself included, you'll never forget the experience

great wash-tubs of crabs are steamed and eaten, usually at picnic-type tables covered with newspapers. the dainty little utensils employed are wooden clubs or mallets (for cracking claws) and a sharp knife. since the crabmeat that is extracted from the shell is most often well laced with cayenne and other nice spices, a plentiful supply of beer is essential

if you are a crab fancier, you will find it hard to stop eating—and before the evening is over, you might well discover that you have put away 6 or 8—or even more!

if you'd like to cook up a modest little feast of your own, for kitchen or backyard, here's what you do:

take a large pot or kettle and arrange somehow to fit a grill in it a couple of inches from the bottom. pour in a cup of vinegar, 2 cups of water, 1 tablespoon black pepper, 1 tablespoon dry mustard, and 1 teaspoon cayenne. add 1 teaspoon curry powder, mace or a mixture called "crab boil," if you wish. turn the heat up, and when steam begins to rise, toss in 2 dozen crabs one at a time (so that you can be sure they're alive) and clamp the lid on tight. the crabs will cook in about 10 minutes—they're done when they are pink. the grill will keep them from getting water-logged in their own juices. open them, crack them, pick them (see index), and eat them—and don't forget the beer! (you should have enough to serve 4, if the crabs are large enough)

FRIED SOFT-SHELL CRABS

8 live soft-shell crabs
2 eggs, beaten
1/4 cup milk
2 teaspoons salt
1/2 cup flour
1/2 cup dry bread crumbs
cooking oil

kill the crabs by cutting off the face. lift the top shell and remove the gills and digestive organs. rinse in cold water and drain

combine the egg, milk, and salt

combine the flour and crumbs, dip the crabs in the egg mixture, roll in the flour-crumb mixture, and fry over moderate heat in a heavy skillet with 1/8 inch cooking oil until brown

turn and brown other side

(4 servings)

or, you can deep-fat fry them (see index)
or, you can dust the crabs lightly with flour and pan fry them in butter

CREAMED CRABMEAT

2 tablespoons butter
2 tablespoons flour
1 cup cream
2 hard-cooked eggs, chopped
1/2 teaspoon salt
1/2 teaspoon pepper
1 teaspoon paprika
dash cayenne
1 teaspoon sherry
1 pound cooked crabmeat
toast or patty shells

make a roux, stirring the flour smoothly into the melted butter

add the cream, chopped eggs, seasonings, and cook until smooth and thickened

add the crabmeat, cook a minute or so, remove from the heat, stir in the sherry. serve on toast points or patty shells

(4 servings)

CRAB AND MUSHROOM CASSEROLE

2 tablespoons butter
1 cup chopped mushrooms
1 tablespoon flour
1/2 cup cream
1 pound crabmeat
juice of 1/2 lemon
1 teaspoon capers
1 teaspoon chopped parsley
2 egg whites, beaten stiff

sauté the mushrooms gently in the butter until tender, stir in 1 tablespoon flour, cook for a minute or two, and add the cream

stir until thickened, then add the crabmeat, lemon juice, capers, and egg whites

place into a buttered casserole and cook in a preheated 350° oven for about 20 minutes

(6 servings)

this is delicious, even using canned crabmeat

king crab

blue crab

dungeness crab

CRAWFISH

The crawfish (British spelling: crayfish) is a small freshwater lobster ranging from 3-1/2 to 6 or 7 inches long. Cultivated in aerated fresh water ponds, the little creatures are marketed fresh and frozen to enthusiasts in France and the Scandinavian countries and to the restaurants of New Orleans, New York, and other cities.

Crawfish tails may be served hot with a variety of sauces or the whole animal may be cooked (with dill) and served cold.

Many shrimp recipes may be adapted to the preparation of crawfish, but there is one really great dish that must be included here:

CRAWFISH, NANTUA

here is one of the great dishes of gourmet France. we had it at Hôtel de la Poste, Beaune, in the heart of the Burgundy wine country of France. I had had a letter of introduction to the owner, Marc Chevillot, who turned out also to be the chef, and I must say we received royal treatment. this is the recipe as close as I can come. I have tried it since but having no crawfish, I used jumbo gulf shrimp instead. it wasn't quite the same dish

2 pounds crawfish, fresh or frozen

2 cups fish stock (see index)

1/2 cup béchamel sauce (see index)

1/2 cup cream

pinch cayenne

2 tablespoons butter

1 tablespoon finely chopped shallots

1/2 teaspoon salt

pinch cayenne

3 tablespoons cognac

1/2 cup hollandaise sauce (see index)

put the crawfish into a pot with the fish stock, cover, and steam over high heat for 5 minutes or until crawfish are pink

remove the crawfish, let cool a little, slit the tails, and remove the meat. set aside

to 1 cup of the liquid, strained, add 1/2 cup béchamel sauce, 1/2 cup cream, and cayenne, cook, stirring over high heat until the sauce is reduced to half

in a heavy skillet heat 2 tablespoons butter, add the shallots, salt, cayenne, and crawfish tails, heat, stirring until

(continued)

warmed through, then add the cognac, ignite, and stir well

pour the sauce over the crawfish, cook, stirring for a minute or so

remove from the heat, stir in the hollandaise sauce, transfer to 4 gratin dishes, and brown for 1 minute or so under the broiler

(4 servings)

CROAKER

A lean fish found along the Atlantic Coast in waters of moderate temperature, the croaker—because of its small size—is best suited for pan-frying like freshwater bass (see index).

EELS

There are many species of eel and they are found in all kinds of waters.

The common American eel, like the freshwater eel of Europe, spends most of his life in a river, lake, or pond, then each spring swims out into the sea to spawn (reversing the habit of most fish such as salmon, shad, herring, and even other eels that live at sea and spawn in the rivers).

This eel attains a length of 2 to 4 feet, has a viscous, slippery skin and firm, delicate flesh (unless he has spent a lazy life in stagnant waters, in which case the flesh is soft and slimy).

The moray and the conger, two of the best known of the sea eels, grow much larger and are used chiefly in bouillabaisse and stews.

The lamprey—not a true eel, although very much like one in appearance—lives at sea and spawns in the river like most other self-respecting fishes.

Eels are marketed frozen, smoked, iced, or live in fish tanks. In any case, the unpleasant job of cleaning an eel is usually taken over by the fishmonger. Should you be confronted with the problem, however, follow these steps: (1) sock him in the head and kill him; (2) hang him up by a string tied around his neck; (3) make a shallow circular incision below the string; (4) grab the skin with pincers or a cloth and tear down; (5) slit along the belly, eviscerate, decapitate, and remove the coating of fat between flesh and skin; (6) cut into slices, fillets, chunks, or leave whole, depending upon size and recipe. Nothing to it!

Eels may be poached, broiled, fried, or smoked—served hot as a main dish or cold as an appetizer.

FRIED MARINATED EELS

**3 pounds eels, cleaned
and cut into 4-inch pieces
court-bouillon #1
(see index)
1 egg, well beaten
1/2 cup olive oil
1 cup dry bread crumbs
(or cracker crumbs)
salt
pepper
chopped parsley**

place the eel pieces into a stainless steel or enamel skillet, nearly cover with court-bouillon, let stand for an hour, then poach at low heat for about 20 minutes

beat the egg and a teaspoon of olive oil until foamy

dip the eel pieces first into the egg-oil mixture, then into bread cumbs, and fry until golden in hot olive oil

season with salt and pepper and serve garnished with chopped parsley

(4 servings)

BROILED EELS WITH DILL

**3 pounds eels, cleaned and
cut into 4-inch pieces
1/2 cup olive oil
1 teaspoon paprika
fresh dill
salt
pepper**

heat the olive oil, add the paprika and dill

dip the eel pieces into the hot oil, season with salt and pepper, place on the broiler rack, and cook for 10 minutes on each side until golden brown and flaky when fork-tested. brush frequently with oil during the process

serve garnished with a little of the dill, chopped

(4 servings)

DEEP-FRIED BRANDIED EELS

3 pounds eels, cleaned and cut into 4-inch pieces
juice of 1 lemon
3 tablespoons cognac
2 teaspoons salt
1/2 teaspoon pepper
1 egg, well beaten
1/2 cup milk
1 cup flour
fat for deep frying
chopped dill or parsley

combine the lemon juice, cognac, 1 teaspoon salt, and 1/2 teaspoon pepper, and marinate the eels in this mixture for an hour or so, turning often

combine the egg and milk, sprinkle in the flour, add a teaspoon of salt, and mix into a smooth batter

dip the eel pieces into the batter and fry 2 or 3 at a time in deep fat until golden brown

serve garnished with chopped dill

(4 servings)

THE FLATFISHES

Perhaps the most universally popular of all food fishes, the flatfishes abound in all kinds of marine waters, some even venturing into fresh water streams. There are more than 500 known species. Although they vary greatly in size, all flatfishes are characterized by having both eyes on one side—some on the left and some on the right. The young are born with normally placed eyes but as they develop, one eye crosses over the top of the head and settles beside the other. At the same time that side of the fish becomes the top side and takes on protective coloration matching the ocean bottom.

The following are the best-known species:

species	weight (*pounds*)	home waters	characteristics
brill	2 to 8	European	eyes on L, tiny scales
chicken halibut	25 to 50	Pacific	eyes on R, greenish-brown, scaleless
Dover sole	up to 2	European	eyes on R, olive brown, small scales
fluke (summer flounder)	2 to 8	Atlantic	eyes on L, light greenish-brown, large mouth
gray sole (a flounder)	2 to 8	Atlantic & European	eyes on L, brownish-gray, small scales
gulf flounder	up to 2	Gulf	eyes on L, mottled gray-brown
halibut	300 to 400	Atlantic	eyes on R, dark brown, scaleless, largest of all flatfishes
lemon sole (a flounder)	up to 4	Atlantic	eyes on R, gray-brown
rusty dab	up to 2	Atlantic & Pacific	eyes on R, greenish-brown rusty red dots
starry flounder	6 to 12	Pacific	eyes on L, or R, star-shaped blotches
turbot	6 to 12	European	eyes on L, tiny scales, largest of European flatfish
winter flounder	up to 5	Atlantic	eyes on R, reddish-brown, thicker than most

Recipes for all the varieties of flatfish flounder, except halibut and turbot—fluke, gray sole, lemon sole, gulf flounder, starry flounder, etc.—are given under *sole* (see index).

GRAYLING

found in the clear streams and lakes of the upper Missouri River basin, and weighing from 1 to 2 pounds, the grayling is a close relative of the trout. So cook it the same way you would a trout

---

GROUPER

the grouper, a sort of warm-water sea bass, runs large, often weighing 50 pounds or more. This is the slow, friendly, colorful fish you encounter while snorkling or glass-bottom-boat exploring in Bermuda and Caribbean waters. In the markets you encounter a much smaller species sold to you as steaks or fillets

---

GRILLED GROUPER STEAK

2 pounds grouper steak (or steaks) about 3/4 inch thick
1/2 cup dry vermouth
1/2 cup salad oil
1 tablespoon lemon juice
1/2 teaspoon salt
few peppercorns
pinch thyme
1 tablespoon chopped parsley
lemon wedges

place the steak into a shallow glass dish, add the remaining ingredients, and marinate at room temperature for 3 hours, turning once

remove the steak, place on an oiled broiler rack, broil under high heat until brown, brushing frequently with the marinade. turn and repeat until fish flakes with a fork, or about 15 minutes

serve with lemon slices

(4 servings)

you can do this one over a charcoal broiler—and you can use almost any kind of fish steaks

SCALLOPED HADDOCK AU GRATIN

2 pounds haddock fillets, cut into cubes
2 tablespoons butter
1/2 green pepper, minced
1/2 onion, minced
1 teaspoon salt
pinch white pepper
1 cup milk
2 tablespoons flour
1/2 teaspoon Worcestershire
1/2 cup grated cheese (cheddar is best) mixed with 1/2 cup bread crumbs

melt the butter in a saucepan, add the green pepper, onion, salt, pepper, and haddock cubes

cook gently over low heat about 10 minutes

shake milk and flour together until well blended, add Worcestershire, and pour into the saucepan with the haddock. stir-cook for 10 minutes and remove to a buttered ovenproof dish

sprinkle with the cheese-bread crumbs mixture and place under the broiler until golden (4 servings)

HADDOCK FILLETS, MUSHROOM SAUCE

2 1/2 pounds haddock fillets
1/2 teaspoon salt
pinch pepper
pinch cayenne
1 tablespoon flour
1 tablespoon butter
1 tablespoon cooking oil
1 1/2 cups mushroom sauce (see index)
1 teaspoon chopped fresh dill

pat the fillets dry with a paper towel, season on both sides with salt, pepper, and cayenne, and dust lightly with flour

place butter and oil into a heavy skillet, heat, add the fillets one at a time, and brown on both sides

remove to a preheated serving platter, pour mushroom sauce over the top, and serve garnished with chopped fresh dill (4 servings)

HAKE

a cousin of the cod, hake is often caught in the same nets. Any recipe good enough for cod is good enough for hake

---

HALIBUT AND TURBOT

These two cousins, the largest of the flatfish family (sole, flounder, fluke, dab, etc.) are among the most prized gastronomically of all seafood. Both have tiny-scaled tough skin and eyes on the same side of the body (the halibut on the right, the turbot on the left), but the halibut can grow to a length of 10 feet—and often does—while the turbot rarely exceeds 30 inches.

The flesh of these two fish is peculiarly similar—white, firm, flaky, lean, and delicately flavored—yet they have never met. The halibut, strictly an American, wouldn't be caught in European waters, and no turbot worthy of the name has ever been found outside of Europe.

We had *turbot au champagne* at Laserre, one of Paris' great restaurants. I was unable to come away with the recipe, but you could make a rough copy of the dish by poaching turbot fillets in a good court-bouillon and serving them with a champagne velouté sauce and topping with sliced truffles. But you'd have to substitute chicken halibut unless you came upon turbot fillets flown in from Europe.

HALIBUT À LA DIABLE

1 1/2 pounds halibut steaks
steamed (see index) and
flaked
2 tablespoons cream
1 cup mayonnaise
2 tablespoons chili sauce
2 teaspoons prepared
mustard
2 drops Tabasco sauce
1/2 teaspoon vinegar
1/2 teaspoon paprika
1/2 teaspoon celery salt

combine all the ingredients
and mix well

place 4 slices buttered toast
onto a baking sheet, cover with
the halibut mixture, and bake
in a preheated 350° oven for
15 minutes or until brown

(4 servings)

FRIED HALIBUT BITS

1 teaspoon salt
1 cup flour
1 teaspoon baking
powder
1 teaspoon marjoram
1/2 teaspoon salt
1/4 teaspoon pepper
1 egg beaten with
3/4 cup milk
2 pounds halibut steaks,
skin and bone removed
fat for deep frying

sift together the flour, baking
powder, marjoram, salt, and
pepper, and combine with the
egg-milk mixture to form a
batter

cut steaks into 1 1/2-inch
cubes, season with salt, dip
into the batter and fry in deep
fat

(6 servings)

HALIBUT À LA POULETTE

1/2 cup butter salt freshly ground pepper 1 tablespoon lemon juice 1 tablespoon grated onion 2 1/2 pounds halibut, cut into 8 thin slices flour 2 cups béchamel sauce (see index) 2 hard-cooked eggs, finely chopped	melt the butter, season with salt and pepper, add the lemon juice and onion dip the halibut slices into this mixture, roll, fasten with toothpicks, place into a shallow pan, and sprinkle lightly with flour. bake in a preheated 350° oven for 15 minutes place the slices on a serving platter, remove toothpicks, pour the béchamel sauce around them and garnish with chopped egg (4 servings)

alternate steaks: salmon, swordfish, catfish, and lingcod

CURRIED HALIBUT CASSEROLE

1 package (8 ounces) cooked noodles 1 1/2 pounds halibut steaks, steamed (see index) and flaked 1 1/2 teaspoons curry powder 2 tablespoons melted butter 1/2 cup milk 1 can (10 ounces) cream of mushroom soup 1 cup grated cheese	place the cooked noodles into greased casserole, cover with the flaked fish steaks combine the curry, butter, milk, and soup. add to the casserole, sprinkle with cheese, and bake in a preheated 350° oven for half an hour (6 servings)

CALIFORNIA HALIBUT ROAST

thick slice halibut
(about 2 1/2 pounds)
2 tablespoons melted
butter
2 tablespoons fish stock
or
2 tablespoons fumet
salt
freshly ground pepper
1 cup cream, sweet or sour
1 tablespoon chopped
shallots (or scallions)
1 tablespoon chopped
parsley

wipe the steak with a paper towel, spread both surfaces with butter, and place in a shallow baking dish

moisten with fumet or a good fish stock (see index), season with salt and pepper, and bake in a preheated 375° oven for 15 minutes

remove skin and center bone, add the cream and chopped shallots, and cook for 15 minutes longer

garnish with parsley and serve in the baking dish

(6 servings)

alternate steaks: cod, muskellunge, lingcod, swordfish

HERRING

Excellent in flavor, high in food value, low in cost, this versatile fish can be found in markets all over the world in almost every possible form—salted, smoked, pickled, kippered, canned, fresh, and frozen. The young are packaged and sold as sardines—the roe is canned.

The people of all nations go for it. The Scotch, English, and Irish kipper it and eat it for breakfast. The Scandinavians, who can't get along without it, eat herring in any form and at any meal. The Dutch, the Germans, the Jews, include it in their diet regularly. American slaves in Virginia and Maryland found herring a welcome addition on the menu to side meat, "chittlins," and corn pone.

When I was young, there always seemed to be a wooden tub of Potomac River salt herring out in the back yard which ended up on the breakfast table to be eaten with pancakes.

If it were a rare fish, herring would, without a doubt, be considered a gourmet's delicacy.

Herring may be fixed almost any way. It may be grilled, fried, broiled, sautéed, or stewed.

The Norwegians eat it "raw." The Irish smoke it, split it, douse it with whisky, and set it afire. But, however you cook herring, if it's salted, be sure first to soak the salt out with several changes of water or milk.

LINGCOD STEAKS, MUSHROOM STUFFING

2 tablespoons butter
1/4 cup chopped shallots (or onions)
1/2 cup chopped raw mushrooms
1/4 cup minced parsley
1/4 teaspoon thyme
1/2 cup fresh bread crumbs
1/4 cup cream
salt
pepper (preferably white)
2–1 1/2 pound lingcod steaks
paprika
lemon slices

using a skillet, cook the shallots at low heat in butter until soft, then add the mushrooms, parsley and thyme and cook 5 minutes longer

mix the bread crumbs and cream, season to taste with salt and pepper, and mix well with the onion and mushrooms

make a sandwich of the two steaks with the stuffing between and place into a buttered baking dish. bake in a preheated 425° oven for about 20 minutes or until fish flakes with a fork, keeping moist with fumet (see index) or melted butter

dust with paprika and serve with lemon slices

(6 servings)

LOBSTERS

Largest of the crustaceans, the lobster is found in the cold waters of the North Atlantic from Labrador to North Carolina, but by far the bulk of the catch is made along the coasts of Maine and Massachusetts. A European species differing somewhat in size, shape, and coloration is found in the Northern European waters.

The lobster reaches full growth slowly, more than six years being required to produce the minimum legal marketable size. Although creatures have been taken weighing 20 pounds or more, in the market they weigh from 1 to 3 pounds—are graded as *chickens* (3/4 to 1 pound), *quarters* (1 1/4 pounds), *large* (1 1/2 to 2 1/4 pounds) and *jumbo* (over 2 1/2 pounds).

Lobsters are sold live, cooked in the shell, or frozen. Lobster meat cooked and removed from the shell is available iced, frozen, or canned.

The warmer waters of the world—the Mediterranean, the Caribbean, the Gulf of Mexico, and the warmer oceans produce a totally different creature called a Spiny or Rock lobster, a sort of marine crawfish lacking the large claws of the cold-water species. The color, markings, and texture of these lobsters differs from region to region, and experts can tell their habitat with reasonable accuracy—South Africa, rough maroon shell, no spots; Southern California and Mexico, smooth shells red to orange in color, etc. . . . The meat, firm but a little tough, is located almost entirely in the tail. Severed and frozen, these lobster tails have in recent years gained wide popularity in the market.

In the recipes that follow, the meat of either lobster may be used unless otherwise specified.

STEAMED LOBSTER

many New Englanders decry the practice of boiling a lobster, holding that the meat is rendered soggy by unnecessary contact with water. For these the favored process is cooking by steam. Follow the directions for steaming crabs (see index)

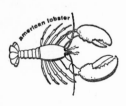
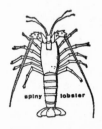

BROILED LOBSTER

**4 live lobsters,
1 1/2 pounds each
4 tablespoons butter
1/2 teaspoon salt
1/2 teaspoon white
pepper
1/2 teaspoon paprika
lemon wedges
melted butter**

kill the lobsters by inserting the point of a knife between the body and the tail sections. cut in half lengthwise, removing the stomach (just in back of the head), and the intestinal vein. crack the claws

place lobsters onto a broiler pan, brush with butter, sprinkle with salt, pepper, and paprika and broil about 4 inches from the heat for 12 to 15 minutes or until lightly browned

garnish with lemon wedges and serve with melted butter (4 servings)

broil spiny lobster tails the same way

BOILED LOBSTER

4 live lobsters
(1 1/2 pounds each)
4 quarts boiling water
6 tablespoons salt
lemon wedges
melted butter

plunge lobsters head first into boiling salted water* and continue cooking for 20 minutes. drain

cut in half lengthwise, remove the stomach (just back of the head), and the intestinal vein

eat and enjoy hot or cold with melted butter and lemon

(4 servings)

STUFFED LOBSTER

4 live lobsters,
1 1/4 pounds each
3 cups soft bread cubes
4 tablespoons butter,
melted
2 tablespoons grated
onion
1 clove garlic, minced

cook and clean the lobsters (see index), remove, and save the green liver and coral

mix together the bread cubes, butter, onion, garlic, liver, and coral. place in the body cavities and spread over the tail meat

place into a shallow baking pan or baking sheet and bake in a preheated 400° oven for 20 to 25 minutes or until golden

(4 servings)

add a cup of grated cheese to the stuffing for a variation

* or place them in cold water and bring the water to a boil. Scientific experiments made to ascertain which is the more humane way to kill a lobster revealed the following surprising results: lobsters placed in cold water appeared to expire gradually and painlessly as the temperature of the water increased, while those plunged alive into boiling water made violent attempts to escape, remaining alive up to a full minute

LOBSTER NEWBURG

A very famous dish first introduced to the gastronomic world by a very famous restaurant—Delmonico's.

Originally, Lobster Newburg was called Lobster à la Wenberg after Ben Wenberg, sea captain and gourmet, who took most of his meals at Delmonico's when not at sea, and who invented the method of preparing lobster. Alas, Charles Delmonico and Ben had a falling out and Charley changed the name of this, his most popular offering, to Newburg (*new* being *wen* spelled in reverse). This all took place back in the 1890's.

In 1939 at the New York World's Fair, I watched George Rector make Lobster Newburg. Here's the great man's recipe, and I quote:

"Select a live lobster weighing about two pounds and plunge it into boiling salted water to cook for twenty minutes. Remove from water and when cool cut and break open the shell and remove the lobster meat and cut it into pieces about the size of a small walnut. Now melt two tablespoons of fresh butter and cook the pieces of lobster in it for several minutes then season with salt and a few grains of cayenne pepper and four tablespoons of sherry wine . . . cook one minute and add one cup of heavy cream and the yolks of two eggs slightly beaten. Stir gently but do not allow to boil after yolks have been added. Serve with triangles of fresh toast."

Orally, he added an alternate version which I have never heard of since. It consisted of substituting a little thick béchamel sauce and two tablespoons of hollandaise for the cream and egg yolk.

Today you don't have to go through the live lobster bit; you can use cooked canned lobster meat, frozen lobster tails, or even shrimp.

LOBSTER THERMIDOR

George Rector is credited with bringing this famous dish from France to his father's restaurant in New York during the early 1900's. up to that time, it had been an exclusive offering of the *Café de Paris* in Paris

4 live lobsters, 1 1/4 pounds each
1/2 cup melted butter
1 cup chopped mushrooms, fresh or canned
1/2 teaspoon salt
1/2 teaspoon freshly ground pepper
1 teaspoon English mustard
1 tablespoon Worcestershire sauce
few grains cayenne pepper
1/2 cup sherry
1/4 cup cognac
1 1/2 cups heavy cream
3 egg yolks, beaten
1/2 cup bread crumbs
1/2 cup grated Parmesan cheese
paprika

cook and clean the lobsters (see index), remove the meat and cut into 1/2-inch pieces. reserve the shells

gently sauté the mushrooms in half the butter for two minutes

off the heat, add the lobster meat, seasonings, sherry, cognac, cream, egg yolks, and bread crumbs. mix well

fill the lobster shells with this mixture, pour on the remaining butter, and dust with cheese and paprika

place on a shallow pan or baking sheet and bake in a preheated 400° oven for 10 minutes or until brown

(4 servings)

the restaurants of Bermuda glamorize the not-too-tasty spiny lobsters from the local Gulf Stream waters by serving them *thermidor*

LOBSTER À L'AMÉRICAINE

you can get into a quick argument over the origin and name of this superlative dish. was it created in America or in France? was it named after Americans who are reported to be great tomato lovers, or is the name *à l'Américaine* a transcription—deliberate or otherwise—of *à l'Armoricaine* (Armorica being Brittany)? these dichotomous arguments don't affect me one wit; I will always be happy just to eat lobster *à l'Américaine*—or is it *à l'Armoricaine*?

2 live lobsters, 1 1/4 pounds each (hen lobsters are better)
1/4 cup olive oil
4 tablespoons butter
3 tablespoons finely chopped shallots (or onions)
1 clove garlic, minced
4 fresh tomatoes, peeled, seeded, and squeezed
2 tablespoons tomato paste
2 tablespoons chopped fresh parsley
1 tablespoon chopped fresh tarragon
few grains cayenne
1/2 teaspoon salt
1/4 cup warmed cognac

kill the lobsters by stabbing them in the back between the body and the tail. cut off the legs and claws and crack the claws. slice the tails at the joints. split the carcass in two lengthwise, remove, and discard the gritty substances behind the head. remove and save the coral and liver

heat the oil in a heavy skillet, toss in the lobster pieces and cook-stir until the shells are pink and the meat browned. then remove to a heated platter

add the butter, shallots, and garlic to the skillet, and simmer gently for a minute or two

add the tomatoes, tomato paste, parsley, tarragon, cayenne, salt, and wine. cover and simmer for half an hour

pour the cognac over the lobster pieces, ignite, then add them to the sauce, cover, and cook 15 minutes longer. just before serving, add the coral and liver

(4 servings)

MACKEREL

The mackerel family of fishes comprises one of the most prolific and varied in the sea, ranging all the way from tiny "sardines" to albacore and tuna. Those most commonly displayed in markets are the so-called Boston mackerel, weighing about a pound, Spanish mackerel, from 2 to 3 pounds, and king mackerel (sometimes known as kingfish). The flesh of all varieties is firm and sweet but somewhat oily, so the fish is at its best when broiled or served with a spicy sauce.

KINGFISH (KING MACKEREL) STEAK VINAIGRETTE

thick slice kingfish
(about 2 1/2 pounds)
4 tablespoons butter
1/2 cup fish stock
1/2 cup sauce vinaigrette
(see index)
salt
paprika

melt the butter in a heavy skillet, add the steak, fish stock, and sauce, seasoning to taste

poach about 10 minutes on each side or until fish flakes with a fork, basting frequently

garnish with paprika and serve

(4 servings)

alternate steaks: black sea bass, grouper, fresh tuna

mackerel

MACKEREL STEAK, CURRY SAUCE

thick slice king mackerel
(about 2 1/2 pounds)
1 cup fish stock
1 onion, finely chopped
1/2 green pepper,
finely chopped
1 stalk celery,
finely chopped
1 teaspoon curry powder
dash Tabasco sauce
3 tablespoons flour
salt
pepper
1 cup dry white wine
or French vermouth
2 tablespoons chopped
parsley

poach the halibut in the stock for 15 minutes, remove skin and center bone, and set aside on a serving platter and keep warm

to the stock add the onion, pepper, celery, curry powder, and Tabasco, cook at low heat for 10 minutes

thicken with flour, season with salt, and pepper, and cook 5 minutes longer

add the wine, stir, pour over the steak, and serve garnished with chopped parsley

(6 servings)

MULLET

A. a gray or striped fish with a cylindrical body found along the coast of the middle and southern part of the United States with a firm, tender flesh containing a yellowish, mild-flavored oil. The fish is marketed whole, in sizes ranging from 1/2 pound to 3 pounds, filleted in larger sizes, and smoked in all sizes

B. a freshwater fish found in streams and lakes all over the United States, ranging in size from 2 to 5 pounds, and marketed whole or filleted, fresh, frozen, salted, or smoked. The meat is firm, sweet, flaky, and contains, like its saltwater cousin, a delicately flavored oil

C. a delicious red fish found in the Mediterranean Sea (called by the French *rouget*). The fish is grilled, fried, or baked (but never steamed or boiled). Great care is taken in cleaning the fish to leave the liver (a great delicacy) intact. In fact, some cooks remove only the scales, leaving the entrails, also, intact

the European mullet is unavailable on this side of the Atlantic

the American mullet, both marine and freshwater, are bottom feeders, and under certain conditions taste a little of their muddy habitat, in which case they should be marinated before cooking

---

MARINATED MULLET FILLETS

2 1/2 pounds freshwater mullet fillets, skinned
1/2 cup olive oil
1/4 cup vinegar
2 teaspoons salt
1/4 teaspoon pepper
1 onion, sliced
1/2 teaspoon thyme
1 onion, minced
bread crumbs
minced parsley

mix the oil, vinegar, seasonings, and spices, and marinate the fillets for an hour or more using a shallow glass dish

drain and place the fillets into a greased baking dish, sprinkle with minced onion and bread crumbs, and bake in a preheated 400° oven for half an hour or until flesh flakes when fork-tested

serve garnished with minced parsley

(4 servings)

GRILLED MULLET, ANCHOVY BUTTER SAUCE

1 saltwater mullet (about 4 pounds), dressed
1 teaspoon salt
1/2 teaspoon pepper
anchovy butter (see index)
chopped watercress

make a few shallow cuts across the mullet, season with salt and pepper, and place onto a greased rack, and brush with anchovy butter

broil under a moderate heat for half an hour or until flesh flakes when fork-tested, brushing with anchovy butter frequently

serve garnished with chopped watercress

(6 servings)

BAKED MULLET, MORNAY SAUCE

1 3-pound mullet (fresh or saltwater), dressed
1 teaspoon salt
1/2 teaspoon pepper
1/2 teaspoon paprika
pinch cayenne
mornay sauce (see index)

wipe the fish dry and season inside and out with a mixture of salt, pepper, paprika, and cayenne

place fish into a greased oven pan and bake in a preheated 375° oven for about 40 minutes or until flesh is flaky

transfer to a preheated serving platter, cover with mornay sauce, and serve

(4 to 6 servings)

BAKED MULLET AU GRATIN

1 3-pound mullet (fresh or saltwater), dressed, boned, and cut into serving pieces
1 teaspoon salt
1/2 teaspoon white pepper
1 onion, sliced
3 stalks celery, chopped
1 cup dry white wine
4 tablespoons butter
2 tablespoons flour
1 cup milk
8 tablespoons grated American cheese
2 teaspoons paprika

place mullet pieces into a casserole, season with salt and pepper, cover with onion and celery, and pour in the wine

bake in a preheated 400° oven for 10 minutes

meanwhile melt the butter in a saucepan, stir in the flour, and then the milk, and finally the cheese. blend well

pour the sauce over the mullet pieces, dust with paprika, and bake 10 minutes longer or until fish flakes when fork-tested

serve in the casserole

(4 to 6 servings)

MUSSELS

Mussels are a delicate bivalve with a thin blue-black shell measuring from 2 to 2 1/2 inches long. Found in all the oceans of the world, the best ones come from colder waters. They are also bred commercially in saltwater pools and marketed live in the shell, or canned.

MUSSELS MARINIÈRE

1/4 pound butter
3 tablespoons chopped shallots (or scallions)
pinch thyme
1/4 bay leaf
4 dozen fresh mussels, well scrubbed and debearded
1/2 teaspoon salt
1/2 teaspoon white pepper
1 cup dry white wine
1/2 cup cream mixed with 2 egg yolks
2 teaspoons minced parsley

melt the butter in a large saucepan and gently sauté the shallots, thyme, and bay leaf for a minute or so

add the mussels (only those with tightly closed shells), sprinkle with salt and pepper, and pour on the wine. cover and cook over high heat for 10 minutes or until shells open

remove the mussels to 4 heated soup bowls, strain the liquid, and thicken with the cream-egg yolk mixture

pour the sauce over the mussels, sprinkle with minced parsley, and serve with crusty French bread

(4 servings)

this dish is sometimes made without thickened sauce

MUSSELS PROVENÇALE

follow the recipe for Mussels Marinière with the following exceptions: (1) remove mussels from the shells, (2) dissolve a pinch of saffron in the mussel liquid before thickening, and (3) serve steaming hot over freshly fried croutons

CURRIED MUSSELS

follow the recipe for Mussels Hongroise substituting a teaspoon of curry powder for paprika

MUSSELS HONGROISE

follow the recipe for Mussels Mariniére with the following exceptions: (1) to the strained liquid, add 1/2 cup finely chopped onions that have been sautéed in butter with 2 teaspoons paprika, 3 tablespoons béchamel sauce (see index), and a little cream. (2) cook until thickened and pour over mussels (4 servings)

mussel

FRIED MUSSELS

4 dozen fresh mussels, scrubbed and debearded 1/2 cup olive oil juice of 1 lemon 2 tablespoons chopped parsley 1/2 teaspoon salt 1/2 teaspoon white pepper flour	place the mussels (only those with tightly closed shells) into a saucepan, cover with water, and cook for 10 minutes or until shells open remove mussels from the shells and marinate for 1/2 hour in oil, lemon juice, and parsley drain, season with salt and pepper, dredge with flour, and fry in deep fat (4 servings)

OYSTERS

There has long been speculation about (and admiration for) the man who first had the courage to eat an oyster. But there is no doubt that he lived a long, long time ago, since wall paintings made during the early Grecian and Roman days unmistakably depict the degustation of oysters at banquets and festivals. In all probability, oysters were discovered even before then.

In America, the first settlers arriving on the Eastern shores were delighted to discover large, succulent oysters in great abundance along the coastline and in the bays.

My own discovery of oysters occurred when I was six and a half years old. Standing thigh-deep in the Chesapeake Bay, I was induced to eat them by a playmate, a year older than I (and much more experienced in oceanography). Vernon was the grandson of a freed slave and a native of the Bay country. He knew how to find oysters and would pick them up from the sandy bottom, casually shuck them with his pocket knife, and eat them on the spot.

Oysters, of one sort or another, are found in shallow coastal waters all over the world and range in size from the tiny Olympias of Washington state (thumb-nail size) to the large, rugged, and irregular-shaped Chesapeake Bays. There are Japanese oysters (also cultivated along the Pacific Coast of the United States) and European oysters—smaller, rounder, more regularly-shaped. All have heavy, irregular shells, whitish or grayish in color, with two valves or halves, joined by a hinge which can be tightly closed by a strong muscle, or opened to admit food. The lower valve is heavier and more convex.

During and just after the spawning season, which usually occurs in late spring, oysters, while safe to eat, are thin and watery —thence the taboo against taking them except during the "R" months.

Oysters are nutritious—rich in proteins, minerals, and vitamins —and they are easy to prepare, easy to serve, and can be eaten raw, broiled, fried, scalloped, baked, or stewed.

OYSTER FRY

1 quart shucked oysters
salt
pepper
2 eggs, lightly beaten
2 tablespoons milk or cream
1 cup bread crumbs, cracker crumbs, or cornmeal
cooking fat
butter

drain the oysters, pat them dry with a napkin, and season with salt and pepper

mix the eggs and milk or cream, and dip the oysters into this mixture, and roll in crumbs

fry in a 50–50 mixture of butter and fat for about 5 minutes or until golden brown on both sides. (fat must be heated to the smoking point)

(4 to 6 servings)

or, fry the oysters in deep fat

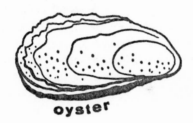

oyster

OYSTERS À LA KING

1 pint shucked oysters
1/4 cup chopped celery
1/4 cup chopped green
pepper
4 tablespoons butter
5 tablespoons flour
2 cups milk
1 egg, beaten
1 tablespoon chopped
pimiento
salt
white pepper

simmer the oysters in their liquor for about 5 minutes or until the edges begin to curl. drain

cook the celery and pepper in butter until tender. sift in the flour and blend, then add the milk, stirring constantly until sauce is thickened

stir a little of the sauce into the beaten egg, then add it and the oysters to the sauce. stir in pimiento and season to taste with salt and pepper. do not boil

serve in patty shells or on toast (6 servings)

Little Neck clams, or chopped cherrystones, may be substituted for oysters, but great care must be taken not to overcook or clams will become tough

OYSTERS AU GRATIN

6 slices buttered toast, cut into quarters and with crusts trimmed
1 pint shucked oysters
1 cup grated cheese
2 eggs, beaten
1 teaspoon salt
1 teaspoon English mustard
1/2 teaspoon paprika
1/2 cup milk

place toast pieces in the bottom of a buttered casserole, cover with a layer of oysters, and sprinkle with grated cheese. repeat with another layer of the same

combine eggs, seasonings, and milk, pour over the casserole, and sprinkle with grated cheese

place casserole in pan of hot water and bake in a preheated 350° oven for half an hour or until brown

(4 to 6 servings)

CREAMED OYSTERS

1 pint shucked oysters
1/2 cup butter
1/2 cup flour
2 cups cream or milk
salt
white pepper

simmer the oysters in their liquor for 5 minutes or until the edges begin to curl. drain

melt butter in the top section of a double boiler, blend in flour, add cream, and cook until thickened, stirring constantly

add oysters, heat, and season to taste, and serve in patty shells or on toast

(4 to 6 servings)

add 1/2 cup sherry and you'll have a dish very much resembling Oysters à la Newburg

OYSTER GRANDE DAME

1 pint shucked oysters
4 tablespoons olive oil
4 tablespoons chopped shallots
4 tablespoons chopped parsley
1 clove garlic, minced
1/2 teaspoon salt
1/2 teaspoon pepper
dash Tabasco sauce
1/2 teaspoon Worcestershire sauce
1 cup dry white wine
flour
2 tablespoons butter

drain the oysters and reserve the liquor

put 2 tablespoons olive oil into a shallow baking dish, add the oysters, and then 2 more tablespoons olive oil

add the herbs, seasonings, the wine, and about half of the oyster liquor

sift a little flour over the top, dot with butter, and bake in a 300° oven for 15 or 20 minutes or until brown on top

serve with good crusty French bread

(4 to 6 servings)

OYSTERS EN BROCHETTE

20 shucked oysters
lemon juice
salt
white pepper
10 strips bacon, cut in half
8 mushroom caps
melted butter
minced parsley

sprinkle the oysters with lemon juice, salt and pepper, and wrap half a bacon strip around each

arrange the bacon-wrapped oysters on 4 skewers (5 on each) with a mushroom cap at each end

brush with butter and grill under a broiler until bacon is crisp

sprinkle with parsley and serve

(4 servings)

OYSTERS ST. PIERRE

1 pint shucked oysters
1 tablespoon butter
1 tablespoon flour
1 cup milk
2 egg yolks, beaten
1/2 onion, finely chopped
1 tablespoon finely
chopped parsley
1/2 cup chopped
mushrooms
1/2 cup chopped
green pepper
1/2 teaspoon salt
1/2 teaspoon pepper
few grains cayenne
1/2 cup dry bread crumbs
butter

simmer the oysters in their liquor for 5 minutes or until the edges begin to curl. drain and chop

melt the butter in the top section of a double boiler, stir in the flour, then the milk, then the egg yolks. mix well

add the seasonings, then the oysters. cook for 2 minutes and transfer to a baking dish, sprinkle top with bread crumbs, dot with butter, and bake for 10 minutes or until brown in a preheated 275° oven

(4 servings)

OYSTER FRITTERS

2 cups flour
1 tablespoon baking
powder
1 1/2 teaspoons salt
2 eggs, beaten
1 cup milk
1 tablespoon melted
butter
1 pint shucked oysters,
drained and chopped
cooking fat

sift the flour, baking powder, and salt together

mix the eggs, milk, and butter together

combine the two mixtures, stir until smooth, and then mix in the oysters

drop the mixture by the spoonful into cooking fat heated to 350° and fry about 3 minutes or until golden

(4 to 6 servings)

chopped clams may be substituted for the oysters

SCALLOPED OYSTERS

2 cups cracker crumbs
1/2 teaspoon salt
1/4 teaspoon white pepper
1/2 cup melted butter
1 pint shucked oysters
1 cup milk
1/2 teaspoon Worcestershire sauce

combine the cracker crumbs, salt, pepper, and butter

sprinkle 1/3 of the mixture into a buttered casserole and cover with 1/2 the oysters, then add another 1/3 of the mixture and the remaining oysters

add the Worcestershire to the milk, pour over the casserole, and cover with the rest of the cracker mixture

bake in a preheated 350° oven for half an hour or until brown

(4 to 6 servings)

PERCH

Perch are one of those small but tasty pan-fry found in the rivers and lakes of the country along with bass, pickerel, crappies, shiners, etc. Since they never, or seldom, reach the commercial markets, the only way you are apt to come by these little fish is by catching them yourself. In cooking them, treat them the same way you would treat any other of the small freshwater fish, such as bass (see index).

A more important species, commercially, is the sea perch caught by New England fishermen from Nova Scotia to Cape Cod. In recent years, these small, firm-fleshed fish, known variously as ocean perch, red perch, rosefish, etc., have become very popular. Filleted, frozen, and packaged, they have been shipped to markets all over the country. When thawed at room temperature for 3 or 4 hours, perch fillets may be poached, broiled, or deep-fried. Follow any of the recipes given for fillets of sole (see index).

PIKE

The pike family of fresh-water fish includes the jack, muskellunge, and pickerel (a much smaller fish). The larger species, found mostly in the Great Lakes, sometimes weigh up to 25 pounds. Those in the market usually weigh only 3 or 4 pounds and are sold whole or filleted, fresh or frozen. The meat is lean, sweet, and firm, but flaky.

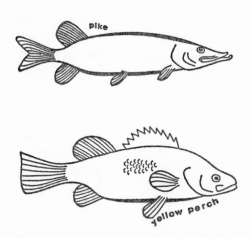

BAKED PIKE WITH SOUR CREAM

2 1/2 pounds pike, dressed
but not split
1 teaspoon salt
1/2 teaspoon pepper
pinch cayenne
1 cup sour cream
1/2 cup grated
American cheese
chopped fresh dill

make several shallow gashes on both sides of the fish and season with salt, pepper, and cayenne

make a thick paste of the sour cream and cheese and spread it on all sides of the fish

place in a greased oven dish and bake in a preheated 350° oven for half an hour or until fish is brown and flakes when fork-tested

serve garnished with chopped fresh dill

(4 servings)

very good way to cook sea bass, too

POLLOCK

The pollock, a relative of the cod, is large and lean. Any recipe good enough for cod will be good enough for pollock.

SAVORY BAKED POLLOCK

3 pounds pollock, dressed, split, and backbone removed
1 teaspoon salt
1/4 teaspoon pepper
pinch cayenne
2 tablespoons butter
2 egg yolks, beaten
2 tablespoons capers
1 onion, minced
2 tablespoons minced parsley
1 teaspoon tarragon vinegar
2 tablespoons cognac
paprika

cut the fish in 4 portions, place into a greased baking dish, season with salt, pepper, cayenne, and butter

bake in a preheated 375° oven for 15 minutes. baste

meanwhile combine the egg yolks, capers, onion, parsley, vinegar, and cognac

mix well, spread evenly over the fish pieces, and dust with paprika

bake 20 minutes longer or until fish flakes when fork-tested

(4 servings)

cod is a similar fish and can be substituted

POACHED POLLOCK STEAKS

2 1/2 pounds pollock steaks
court-bouillon #1 or #2
(see index)
hollandaise sauce
(see index)

place the steaks into a heavy skillet and almost cover with court-bouillon (wrap them in cheesecloth if you wish to prevent breaking them up)

bring to a rapid boil, loosen the fish with a spatula or pancake turner to prevent sticking, lower the heat, and simmer gently for about 20 minutes or until fish is opaque and flaky

remove the steaks carefully and serve topped with hollandaise

(4 servings)

any lean, firm fish steaks may be cooked and served this way

POMPANO

Pompano, abounding in Atlantic and Gulf waters off the Florida coast, is one of the most delicious of all American fishes. The fish averages from 1 1/2 to 3 pounds, has firm, white meat that is delicately fat. Pompano fillets are considered by many the equal in texture and flavor of Dover sole fillets, but unlike sole, they travel poorly and so are not as widely appreciated.

STUFFED POMPANO EN PAPILLOTE

here is a famous dish attributed to Antoine's in New Orleans. it is said to have been created in honor of a now-forgotten but then-famous Brazilian balloonist who was visiting New Orleans. because of the inflated appearance of the cooked papillote, it was originally named Pompano Montgolfier, after the inventor of the balloon. the dish was a favorite of Franklin D. Roosevelt.

I watched Michael Field, the vibrant concert pianist-turned-cook, demonstrate the preparation of pompano fillets en papillote —an exciting dish. try it

4 pompano fillets, about 7 inches long

1/2 cup chicken stock, with fat removed

1/4 cup dry white wine

1 teaspoon salt

2 tablespoons butter

2 tablespoons finely chopped shallots (or scallions)

3 tablespoons flour

2 tablespoons cream

1/2 teaspoon lemon juice

1/2 teaspoon salt

1/8 teaspoon cayenne

1 cup coarsely chopped cooked shrimp

1 cup coarsely diced crabmeat (fresh or canned)

fold the fillets end to end, to prevent breaking, and poach them for about 6 minutes in the chicken stock and wine. remove, unfold, season with salt. reserve

strain the poaching liquid into a saucepan and reduce over high heat to 1 cup. reserve

in another saucepan, cook the shallots in butter for 2 or 3 minutes, stir in the flour, cook for a moment or two, add the reduced poaching liquid and continue cooking until smooth and thick. add the cream, lemon juice, salt, and cayenne. taste for seasonings

cut 4 sheets of parchment cooking paper into 12 by 14 inch heart shapes, fold lengthwise, then open again

lay a fillet on the right half of each papillote, spoon on equal amounts of shrimp and crabmeat on the lower half of each, moisten with a tablespoon of the sauce, fold the top half of the fillet over it, enclosing the stuffing. pour the remaining sauce over each fillet

fold the left half of the parchment over the seal by crimping and rolling the edges together

place the papillotes on a lightly greased cookie sheet and bake in a preheated 450° oven for about 8 minutes

serve in the puffed, browned parchment hearts

(4 servings)

PLANKED POMPANO

1 pompano (about 3 pounds) scaled and drawn, but with head and tail intact
1 teaspoon salt
1/2 teaspoon white pepper
2 cups hot mashed potatoes, seasoned with salt and pepper
2 cups peas, partially cooked
1/4 cauliflower, partially cooked
minced parsley

season fish inside and out with salt and pepper and place onto a hot, buttered hardwood plank

bake in a preheated 350° oven for half an hour or until fish flakes when fork-tested

arrange a border of hot mashed potatoes around the edge of the plank and fill in between potatoes and fish with peas and cauliflower

slide plank into the oven for 5 minutes or until potatoes are browned and vegetables are soft

sprinkle with minced parsley and serve on the plank

(4 servings)

PORGY

The porgy is a small, scaly fish with tender, white flavorful flesh found off the Atlantic Coast from South Carolina to Maine. New Englanders call him a scup, but he is the same fish, averaging from 1 1/2 to 2 pounds and scrappy enough in his own way to interest light-tackle anglers all summer long.

To show you how seriously New Englanders take their scup, a trophy—the Scup Cup—is offered each year by the Nantucket Yacht Club for the season's largest scup and Mitchell's Book Corner, also in Nantucket, will send you instructions on request for cooking your catch.

PORGIES, CHARLESTON STYLE

2 tablespoons olive oil
2 tablespoons butter
1 onion, chopped
2 tomatoes, peeled, seeded, and squeezed dry
1 bay leaf, crumbled
1/2 teaspoon thyme
1 teaspoon salt
1/2 teaspoon pepper
pinch cayenne
4 porgies, dressed
1/4 cup dry sherry
1/2 cup dry bread crumbs

sauté the onions, tomatoes, and seasonings in the oil and butter for 2 or 3 minutes

arrange the porgies in a casserole or baking dish, add the vegetable mixture, and then the wine

bake in a preheated 375° oven for half an hour, or until flesh flakes when fork-tested

sprinkle with bread crumbs and brown quickly under the broiler

(4 servings)

PAN-FRIED SCUP FILLETS

4 porgies, filleted
1 teaspoon salt
1/2 teaspoon white pepper
1/2 cup cornmeal
1/2 cup flour
2 tablespoons cooking oil
2 tablespoons butter
2 tablespoons chopped chives
1 lemon, sliced

wipe fillets with a paper towel and season with salt and pepper

roll the fillets in a mixture of cornmeal and flour

heat the butter and oil in a heavy skillet, add the chives, and then fry the fillets one at a time until golden on both sides

serve with lemon slices

(4 servings)

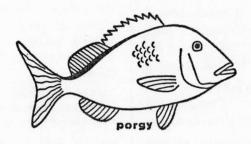

porgy

RED SNAPPER

This fish, one of the choicest delicacies of the sea, averages about 4 pounds and is usually marketed as steaks or fillets, though smaller ones are often sold whole. Found along the Atlantic Coast from Long Island to Brazil, red snapper is most plentiful off the coast of Florida, in the Caribbean Sea, and in the waters off both coasts of Mexico, where it is regarded as the greatest delicacy.

During a recent trip to Mexico, I could scarcely find a major restaurant whose menu did not list red snapper in one form or another. La Cava in Mexico City served it broiled with mustard sauce. Delmonico's listed fillet of snapper *en papillote*. The Rivoli pan-broiled it deliciously. In Acapulco, it was charcoal-broiled whole and served with slices of lime and a moderately hot pepper sauce on the side. The Mayaland out in Yucatan poached little snapper fillets and served them with a cream sauce.

Most of the Caribbean Islands, too, depend heavily on red snapper as a food fish and many of the restaurants prepare it with great imagination.

RED SNAPPER STEAK, GULF STYLE

2 pounds red snapper steak
salt
pepper
2 tablespoons butter
1/2 carrot, chopped
1 stalk celery, chopped
2 tablespoons chopped parsley
6 raw shrimp, chopped
1 cup dry white wine
pinch basil

wipe the steak (or steaks) with a paper napkin, season to taste with salt and pepper, and place in a well buttered casserole

mix all the other ingredients well and pour over and around the fish

bake in a preheated 400° oven for half an hour or until fish steak flakes with a fork

serve in the casserole

(4 servings)

grouper is a very similar fish, although fatter, and can be substituted for red snapper

RED SNAPPER À L'ORANGE

2 1/2 pounds sliced red
snapper
4 tablespoons butter
salt
pepper
2 teaspoons grated orange
rind
1 teaspoon grated
lemon rind
1/2 cup fish fumet
(see index)
4 slices orange

place the snapper into a well
buttered baking pan, season
with salt and pepper, and add
the grated rinds and the fumet
bake in a preheated 350° oven
for half an hour or until fish
flakes when fork-tested, basting occasionally. serve garnished with orange slices

(4 servings)

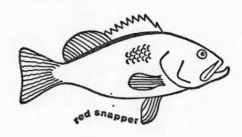

red snapper

Good

RED SNAPPER, CARIBE STYLE

the Mediterraneo, one of the top restaurants in Old Sa...
Puerto Rico, served it in a way I'll never forget. the menu said
Chillo à la Caribe and I ordered it. in due time came a magnificent
fish, nearly a foot long, served whole (head, tail—the works) deep-
fried to a golden brown. the skin was crisp, the meat juicy, the
flavor delicious. the chef—when finally we broke through the language barrier—gave me the following recipe:

**4 small red snappers,
about 1 1/2 pounds each
1 cup lemon juice
2 cups dry white wine
1 clove garlic, split
1 bay leaf, crumbled
3 dashes Tabasco sauce
salt
white pepper
rice flour
peanut oil
coconut oil
minced parsley
1 lemon, quartered**

eviscerate, scale, and defin the
fish, leaving intact the heads
and tails

marinate 3 or 4 hours in the
lemon juice, wine, garlic, bay
leaf, and Tabasco, using a
shallow glass or enamel dish.
turn and baste several times

pat the fish dry, season with *rub olive oil on fish,*
salt and pepper, dust with rice
flour, ~~and deep-fry in a 50-50~~
~~mixture of peanut and coconut~~
~~oil~~

drain and serve at once, garnished with parsley and lemon
wedges *lime*

(4 servings)

*Broil on both sides for a
total of 10 min. per inch of thickness
of fish ≅ 4-6 in from broiler.*

A favorite fish of Bermudans is the rockfish, a close relation to the striped bass found along the Atlantic Coast. One of Bermuda's best restaurants, the Penthouse in Hamilton, serves it this way:

ROCKFISH, PARISIENNE

4 rockfish fillets
(about 3/4-pound each)
court-bouillon #1
(see index)
white wine and egg sauce
(see index)
minced parsley

poach (see index) the fillets in court-bouillon until firm and fork-flaky

transfer to warm platter, spoon on the white wine sauce, garnish with minced parsley, and serve

(4 servings)

DEVILED ROCKFISH

2 pounds rockfish fillets
1 teaspoon salt
2 cups dry bread crumbs
1 teaspoon dry mustard
2 tablespoons minced parsley
2 hard-cooked eggs, chopped
1/2 cup melted butter
2 tablespoons lemon juice
1/2 cup catsup
few dashes Tabasco sauce

wipe fillets dry, season with salt, and set aside

mix all the remaining ingredients into a well-blended paste

place half the fillets into a greased baking pan, cover with half of the mixture. place the other fillets on top and cover with the remaining paste

bake in a 375° oven for half an hour or until flaky

(4 servings)

BAKED ROCKFISH, NEWBURG

2 pounds rockfish fillets
1 teaspoon salt
1/2 teaspoon pepper
1 tablespoon butter
1 onion, minced
2 cups Newburg sauce
(see index)
chopped dill

season the fillets with salt and pepper, place into a buttered oven dish and sprinkle with minced onion

bake in a preheated 375° oven for half an hour or until fish flakes when tested with a fork

remove to a heated serving platter, cover with Newburg sauce, and serve garnished with chopped dill

(4 servings)

FLAKED ROCKFISH BÉCHAMEL

1 1/2 pounds rockfish,
steamed (see index) and
flaked
2 tablespoons butter
3 teaspoons flour
pinch cayenne
1 cup clam broth
or fish stock
2 egg yolks, beaten
1 tablespoon chopped dill
4 slices toast

melt the butter, stir in the flour, cayenne, and then the clam broth and milk. cook-stir until smooth and thick

add the rockfish and gradually the beaten egg yolks and chopped dill

serve on toast

(4 servings)

substitute any shredded or flaked fish or shellfish

SALMON

Salmon are substantially cold-water fish, found in the northern parts of both the Atlantic and Pacific (and sometimes land-locked in the larger freshwater lakes). Atlantic—or kennebec—salmon, weighing from 10 to 20 pounds are distinguished by their brilliant orange-pink meat. Columbia River and Alaska salmon (called also sockeye and red salmon) smaller in size, have flesh that is deep red in color. A species called chinook is the largest of all.

Salmon, as a food, is widely available everywhere, sold frozen and fresh as steaks, canned, and dried. Smoked salmon that has been pre-salted is known as lox.

SALMON STEAK, PARMESAN

4 salmon steaks about 3/4-pound each
1/4 cup olive oil
1 cup dry white wine, diluted with 1/2 cup water
salt
pepper
1 clove garlic, chopped
1 teaspoon oregano
1/2 cup chopped onions
1/2 cup grated Parmesan cheese
chopped fresh dill
4 lemon slices

oil the steaks well and place side by side in a well buttered baking dish with the wine and water

sprinkle each steak with salt, pepper, garlic, oregano, and chopped onions, top with grated Parmesan cheese, and bake uncovered in a preheated 400° oven about half an hour or until fish flakes when fork-tested

garnish with chopped dill and serve with lemon slices

(4 servings)

if steaks of a fat fish are used (tuna, mackerel, etc.), they need not be oiled

SEATTLE SALMON STEAK

2-pound salmon steak
1 clove garlic, cut
salt
4 tablespoons butter
4 slices raw bacon
1 No. 2 can tomatoes
1 onion, chopped
1 green pepper, chopped
1 bay leaf, crumbled
few grains cayenne pepper

rub the surfaces of the steak with cut garlic, season lightly with salt, place into a buttered casserole, and arrange bacon slices across the top

mix together the tomatoes, onions, pepper, and seasonings, pour over and around the steak, bake in a preheated 400° oven for half an hour or until fish flakes with a fork

(4 servings)

alternate steaks: red snapper, pollock, and swordfish

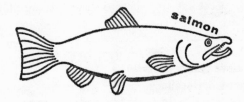

SCALLOPS

The scallop has two shells held together by an adductor muscle like the oyster and clam. But while these latter two creatures just lie on the bottom of the bay and suck in food, the scallop swims through the water or moves about along the bottom. This he does by rapidly opening and closing the shells. Such exercise has the effect, of course, of developing the adductor muscle out of all proportion to the creature itself and it is this portion of the scallop that is prized as food (although Europeans eat the entire scallop).

In the American market only this adductor muscle is available since the scallop, on being caught and removed from the sea, flutters his shells in an attempt to escape captivity. Unlike oysters and clams, the scallop thus loses his life-preserving juices. The meat is therefore removed from the shell and preserved on ice.

Scallops come from the bay, or further out in the sea, those from the bay being smaller and sweeter and tenderer—and more expensive—than sea scallops.

Scallops are easy to prepare and, though never eaten raw, may be cooked almost any way—broiled, baked, creamed, stewed, sautéed, or fried.

SCALLOP FRY

2 pounds bay scallops (or sea scallops sliced in half across the grain)
1/2 teaspoon salt
1/2 teaspoon white pepper
2 eggs, beaten
1 pinch cayenne
1 pinch nutmeg
cracker crumbs
tartar sauce (see index)

season the scallops with salt and pepper and dip them into the egg into which has been beaten the cayenne and nutmeg

roll in cracker crumbs and fry in deep fat

serve with tartar sauce

(4 servings)

OLD-FASHIONED SCALLOP BROIL

1 pound scallops
1 clove garlic, cut
6 tablespoons butter, melted
1/2 teaspoon salt
1/2 teaspoon white pepper
few grains cayenne
flour
1 teaspoon paprika
lemon slices

rub the bottom and sides of a shallow baking dish or pie pan with the garlic, add half the melted butter, and swish around

arrange the scallops in the dish, season with salt, pepper, and a little cayenne, dust lightly with flour and paprika, and pour on the remaining butter

slide under the broiler, cook 10 minutes or until golden, and serve with lemon slices

(4 servings)

SCALLOPS EN BROCHETTE

1 pound scallops
8 slices bacon, quartered
1 clove garlic, crushed
1 scallion, minced
2 tablespoons olive oil
2 tablespoons butter

thread the scallops and bacon slices alternately on skewers and cook under the broiler until brown on all sides

meanwhile in a small saucepan gently sauté the garlic, scallions, and parsley in the oil and butter, without browning

pour the sauce over the skewered scallops

(4 servings)

scallop

BAKED SCALLOPS WITH MUSHROOMS

**4 tablespoons butter
1 cup sliced mushrooms
2 stalks celery, chopped
1 small onion, chopped
1/2 green pepper, chopped
pinch basil
1 pound scallops
2 cups béchamel sauce
(see index)
1/2 cup cracker crumbs
1/2 cup grated cheese**

melt the butter in a saucepan, add the mushrooms, celery, onion, pepper, and basil. simmer gently for 5 minutes

add the scallops and simmer for 5 minutes longer, then add the béchamel. mix well

pour mixture into a buttered casserole. sprinkle on the cracker crumbs, then the cheese

dot with butter and bake in a preheated 325° oven for half an hour

(4 servings)

SCALLOPS IN WINE

**2 tablespoons butter
2 tablespoons olive oil
2 pounds scallops
1/2 teaspoon salt
1/2 teaspoon white pepper
1/2 teaspoon paprika
1 cup dry bread crumbs
chopped fresh dill**

heat the butter and oil in a heavy skillet—to smoking point

season the scallops with salt, pepper, and paprika, and roll in bread crumbs, add to the skillet, and sauté for 5 minutes over high heat, turning to brown evenly

remove the scallops to a heated platter

add the wine to the pan juices, simmer a minute, stirring, and pour over the scallops

serve garnished with chopped dill

(4 servings)

SEA URCHINS

Sea urchins are egg-sized, biscuit-shaped creatures, greenish or black in color, and covered with spines. They are found at low tide on rocks. Almost unknown to American seafood fanciers, they are considered a great delicacy in the region of Marseilles and in the Caribbean.

I have seen them opened and served raw in the markets at Les Halles in Paris and have bought them in the Ninth Avenue fish markets of New York. Usually they are lightly boiled just like an egg in sea water and cut open on the concave side. The excremental parts are discarded and the meat is eaten by dipping in morsels of buttered bread.

SHAD

The shad is a large herring-like migratory fish originally found only in the depths of the Atlantic Ocean but recently introduced into the Pacific. Each spring the fish run up the rivers that flow into the ocean to spawn, the "runs" beginning in February in the rivers of Georgia and the Carolinas and moving northward to the Potomac, Susquehanna, Delaware, Hudson, and Connecticut rivers as spring progresses. Large quantities are caught by gill nets stretched on poles across the rivers.

Averaging from 2 to 5 pounds, shad are considered one of the finest white-flesh fish, although somewhat reproachable for their high oil content and numerous bones. The female are especially prized for their roe.

PAN-BROILED SHAD FILLETS, SAUTERNE

3 pounds shad, filleted
1 teaspoon salt
1/2 teaspoon white pepper
1 cup hot sauterne sauce
(see index)
1 teaspoon minced
parsley

season the fillets with salt and pepper and broil them in a heavy skillet for 5 minutes on each side or until flesh flakes when fork-tested

remove to a heated platter, pour over the hot sauce, and serve sprinkled with minced parsley

(4 servings)

GOLDEN BROILED SHAD FILLETS

3 pounds shad, filleted
1 small onion, grated
2 tablespoons lemon juice
1 teaspoon salt
1/4 teaspoon pepper
1/2 teaspoon paprika
2 tablespoons melted butter
1/8 teaspoon thyme
1/8 teaspoon marjoram
1 tablespoon minced parsley

place the shad fillets on a well greased broiler rack

mix all the other ingredients and brush the fillets with the mixture

cook under the broiler about 7 minutes on each side, brushing frequently with the seasonings

remove when golden brown and serve on a heated platter

(4 servings)

BAKED SHAD, CELERY STUFFING

3 pounds shad, dressed and with backbone removed
1 teaspoon salt
1/2 teaspoon pepper
1 cup celery stuffing (see index)
1 tablespoon minced parsley

make several shallow gashes in both sides of the fish, season with salt and pepper inside and out, and fill loosely with stuffing. skewer or sew

bake in a preheated 375° oven for half an hour or until flesh flakes easily when fork-tested

sprinkle with minced parsley and serve

(4 servings)

BAKED SHAD IN PAPER BAG

3 pounds shad, dressed and with backbone removed
1 teaspoon salt
1/2 teaspoon pepper
2 tablespoons butter, creamed
watercress
lemon slices

season with salt and pepper inside and out. spread with creamed butter, and place into a brown paper bag

preheat the oven to 350°, place the shad in its paper bag in a shallow baking dish and cook for half an hour or until flesh flakes easily when fork-tested

remove from the bag and serve garnished with lemon slices and watercress

(4 servings)

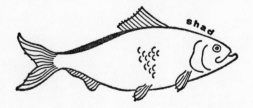

SHEEPSHEAD

The sheepshead, a fish that averages from 3 to 6 pounds, can be found off the Atlantic Coast as far north as Cape Cod and as far south as Florida. Related to the porgy, it appears fresh in Eastern markets during most of the year where it is sold whole or filleted.

Cook sheepshead as you would any marine fish of comparable size.

SHRIMP

Shrimp may well be the most widely liked seafood in the United States—regarded more highly here, in the Caribbean Islands, and in Mexico than in Europe—doubtless because those of American waters are superior, both the dozen-to-the-pound size, found in the depths of the Gulf of Mexico and other southern waters, and the tiny ones from the cold waters of Alaska and New England.

Prawns, found in Dublin Bay and around the Greek Islands are closely related crustacea. Their flavor is good and the flesh is firm, but prawns are short in supply.

Shrimp are readily available in markets all over the country in many forms: whole fresh (with and without the head), frozen raw, frozen cooked, and canned. They cook quickly and easily and can be prepared in a wide variety of ways, and served hot or cold.

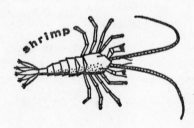

FRIED SHRIMP

1 1/2 pounds raw shelled
shrimp
1 tablespoon cognac
1/2 teaspoon
Worcestershire
1/2 cup flour
pinch salt
1 tablespoon melted
butter
1 egg, beaten
1/2 cup beer
horseradish-marmalade
sauce or tartar sauce
(see index)

brush the shrimp well with a mixture of cognac and Worcestershire

sift the flour and salt together, stir in the butter, egg, and beer until mixture is smooth

dip the shrimp, a few at a time, into the batter and fry in deep fat (see index) until golden

serve with horseradish-marmalade sauce or tartar sauce

(4 servings)

SHRIMP AU GRATIN

1/4 cup butter
1/4 cup flour
1 cup shrimp stock or
fish stock
(see index)
1 cup cream
2 tablespoons sherry
1 1/2 pounds cooked,
shelled shrimp
1 cup grated cheese
salt
pepper

melt the butter in a saucepan, stir in the flour, and cook a minute or so

mix the cream and stock, bring to a boil, add to the butter-flour mixture, stirring until smooth and thickened

add the sherry, the shrimp, and half the cheese. season to taste, place into a shallow baking dish, sprinkle with remaining cheese, and bake in a preheated 375° oven until brown

(4 servings)

SHRIMP NEW ORLEANS

3 tablespoons butter
1 tablespoon flour
1 tablespoon cream
1 cup shrimp stock or
fish stock
(see index)
2 egg yolks, beaten
1 tablespoon chili sauce
1/2 teaspoon salt
pinch cayenne
2 teaspoons minced
onion
1 1/2 pounds tangy
steamed shrimp
(see index), deveined
and deshelled
dry bread crumbs
butter
minced parsley

melt the butter, stir in the flour, let cook for a minute or so, and blend in the cream and stock. simmer 5 minutes and remove from heat

carefully stir in the egg yolks, add the seasonings, and then the shrimp. stir and transfer to 6 ramekins

sprinkle with bread crumbs, dot with butter, and bake in a preheated 375° oven for 5 minutes or until browned

serve garnished with minced parsley

(6 servings)

SHRIMP PATTIES

2 cups cooked, shelled
shrimp
4 slices not-too-fresh
bread, crusts removed
1/4 cup melted butter
containing:
1/2 teaspoon mace
1/2 teaspoon pepper
1/2 teaspoon salt
2 cups béchamel sauce
(see index)

pound the shrimp in a mortar, run them through a meat grinder, or put them into a blender

soak the bread slices, squeeze dry and crumble into the shrimp. mix in the savory butter and shape into small cakes

place in a buttered pan and bake in a preheated 375° oven for 15 minutes or until brown

serve with béchamel sauce

(4 servings)

SHRIMPS LOUISIANA

4 tablespoons butter
2 tablespoons flour
2 onions, finely chopped
1 green pepper, finely chopped
2 fresh tomatoes, peeled and seeded
2 teaspoons chopped parsley
1/2 teaspoon salt
1/4 teaspoon white pepper
pinch cayenne
dash Worcestershire
1 1/2 pounds, shelled raw shrimp
2 teaspoons chopped fresh dill

melt the butter in a saucepan, stir in the flour, then add the onions, pepper, tomatoes, and seasonings, and simmer for 5 minutes or until vegetables are tender

add the shrimp, stir, cover, and simmer for 10 minutes or until shrimp are pink

serve garnished with fresh dill

(4 servings)

SHRIMP PIE

3 slices not-too-fresh bread, crusts trimmed
1 cup milk
1 1/2 pounds cooked, shelled shrimp, coarsely chopped
3 tablespoons butter, melted
1 teaspoon Worcestershire
pinch mace (or grated nutmeg)
1/2 teaspoon salt
1/2 teaspoon pepper
2 tablespoons sherry

soak the bread in the milk and mash with a fork

add the shrimps, butter, and seasonings

put into a buttered casserole and bake in a preheated 375° oven for 20 minutes

(4 servings)

feel free to substitute oysters, lobster, or crabmeat for the shrimp

SHRIMP PILAU

4 slices bacon, quartered 1 onion, chopped 2 cups canned tomatoes 1 cup uncooked rice 1 1/2 pounds cooked, shelled shrimp, coarsely chopped salt pepper	cook the bacon until crisp, re-move and save brown the onion in pan with the bacon fat, add the toma-toes, and simmer for 5 minutes transfer the mixture to the upper section of a double boiler, add the rice, and steam about half an hour or until rice is cooked add the bacon and shrimp, season to taste, and place in a baking dish bake in a preheated 350° oven for about 15 minutes or until rather solid in texture (4 servings)

MEXICAN PAN-BROILED SHRIMP

we had this unforgettable dish on the beach at Acapulco. You don't have to be wearing a bathing suit, sitting under a coconut palm thatch, and drinking the good Mexican beer—but it helps

24 large shrimp, shelled and deveined but with tails intact 1/2 cup lime juice 1/2 cup coconut oil (or olive oil) 4 cloves garlic, chopped 2 or 3 green chilis, peeled and chopped (or 1/2 teaspoon cayenne) 3 tablespoons butter minced parsley	marinate the shrimp overnight in the lime juice, oil, and sea-sonings in a shallow glass or porcelain or stainless steel dish remove the shrimp from the marinade, pan broil in butter for 5 minutes on each side, and serve garnished with minced parsley (4 servings)

TANGY STEAMED SHRIMP

1 stalk celery
1 bay leaf
1/2 clove garlic, chopped
1/2 teaspoon salt
1/2 teaspoon freshly
ground pepper
1/2 cup dry white wine
1 1/2 pounds raw
shrimp in shell
1/2 cup water
melted butter

put celery, seasonings, wine, and water into a saucepan, cover, and simmer gently for 10 minutes

add shrimp, cover, and simmer 5 minutes longer. remove the shrimp and save the stock for use in other shrimp recipes

serve shrimp in the shell with melted butter for dipping

(4 servings)

SHRIMP CURRY

1/4 cup butter
2 onions, chopped
1 clove garlic, crushed
2 cups coconut milk
(or water)
2 tomatoes, peeled and
chopped
1/2 cup chopped celery
1 tablespoon shredded
coconut
1 tablespoon curry powder
1 teaspoon sugar
1 tablespoon flour
1/2 teaspoon salt
1/2 teaspoon pepper
pinch powdered ginger
1 1/2 pounds cooked,
shelled shrimp

gently sauté the onions and garlic in the butter for a minute or two. add the coconut milk, tomatoes, celery, and coconut. bring to a boil

blend the curry powder, sugar, flour, salt, pepper, and ginger. stir in a little water to make a paste and add to the boiling mixture, stirring constantly

cut the heat, cover, and simmer about half an hour. add the shrimp, and continue cooking for 5 minutes longer

serve on rice

(4 servings)

SMELT

Smelt, originally a salt-water fish, was introduced into the Great Lakes around the turn of the century to serve as food for larger lake fish. They thrived, and have become an increasingly important food fish for people.

Each spring, like their marine cousins, these little 7-inch-long fish swarm up the small rivers and streams to spawn where they are literally scooped up by the basket-full by enthusiastic campers and picnickers.

In the market, they are available fresh in season, and frozen almost year around. The meat is sweet, lean and firm.

PAN-FRIED SMELT

16 smelt, cleaned but with heads intact
1 teaspoon salt
1/2 teaspoon pepper
1/2 cup cornmeal
1/2 cup flour
1/2 cup butter
3 tablespoons bacon fat or cooking oil
parsley

wipe the fish dry with a paper towel, season with salt and pepper and roll in a mixture of cornmeal and flour

heat the butter and bacon fat in a heavy skillet until it almost smokes and fry the smelts two or three at a time for about 3 minutes on each side or until golden

serve with parsley

(4 servings)

this is the classic camper's method, borrowed from the American Indian of pan-frying small, fresh-caught fish. It goes for all kinds of small fish—butterfish, spots, brook trout, blowfish, pickerel, croaker, and the small freshwater bass family

SOLE AND FLOUNDER

Sole (Lat. *Solea solea*; Fr. Sole; Ger. *Seezungen*; Sp. *Lenguado*) is the finest of the world's flatfishes.

In shape a long oval, this fish is almost entirely surrounded by fins and is covered with tiny hard scales almost impossible to remove. Sole is found at the bottom of the sea swimming on his side—the left side, which is white. The right, or top side, varies in color, but is generally a protective shade of olive-brown or dirty gray to match the sea bottom over which he swims. Both eyes are placed on this side.

The flesh of sole is white, firm, delicate, digestible, and is easily detached from the bone.

This is the Dover sole—also called English sole. It is found only in European waters but the fish keeps well, and is regularly flown, iced, to the United States.

The American "sole" (lemon sole, gray sole, etc.) belong to the flounder family. Also members of the family are the winter flounder, summer flounder (fluke), northern flounder, southern flounder, starry flounder, black backs, yellowtail, and dabs—all similar in shape, but varying in size, thickness, color, and the position of the eyes which appear on the right in some species, on the left in others.

The flesh of the flounder family is less delicate in flavor than that of Dover sole, less firm, and a little coarser in texture. Fillets cut from these fish are thinner, cook almost too quickly, and are apt to break up easily when handled. For these reasons, it is sometimes a good idea, especially when poaching, to fold or roll them.

Most of the following recipes are written for Dover sole, but almost any flatfish of comparable size (not halibut or turbot)—or even haddock, ocean perch, or other fillets may be freely substituted.

FILLETS OF SOLE DUGLÈRE

4 fillets (about 2 1/2 pounds)

2 tablespoons chopped onion

1 large tomato, peeled, and coarsely chopped

2 tablespoons chopped parsley

1/2 teaspoon salt

1/4 teaspoon white pepper

1/2 cup dry white wine

2 tablespoons butter

2 tablespoons velouté sauce (see index)

few drops lemon juice

2 teaspoons chopped fresh dill

place the fillets into a well oiled oven-proof dish with the onion, tomato, parsley, salt, pepper, and wine. poach gently for a few minutes until fork-flaky. remove the fillets to a serving dish and keep warm

reduce the cooking liquid to about half, add the butter and a few drops lemon juice, and thicken with velouté

cover the fillets with the sauce and serve garnished with chopped dill

(4 servings)

FILLETS OF SOLE ORLY

4 fillets (about 2 pounds)

1/2 teaspoon salt

flour

2 eggs, beaten lightly

bread crumbs

sauce ravigote (see index)

1 lemon, quartered

sprinkle the fillets with salt, roll up, and fasten with toothpicks

roll the fillets first in flour, then in egg, then in bread crumbs

fry in deep fat and serve topped with sauce ravigote and lemon wedges

(4 servings)

FILLETS OF SOLE VÉRONIQUE

4 fillets (about 2 1/2 pounds)
court-bouillon #1 (see index)
5 tablespoons butter
1 1/2 tablespoons flour
salt
pepper
1/4 cup milk
1/4 cup heavy cream
1/2 pound white seedless grapes
2 tablespoons minced parsley

poach the fillets in the court-bouillon and remove to a heated platter

melt 3 tablespoons butter in a small saucepan, stir in the flour until well blended, and then stir in about 3/4 cup of the court-bouillon until thickened

season to taste with salt and pepper, then stir in the milk, cream, 2 tablespoons butter, the grapes, and parsley. pour the sauce over the fillets and serve at once

(4 servings)

FILLETS OF SOLE MARGUÉRY

4 fillets (about 2 1/2 pounds)
court-bouillon #1 (see index)
4 tablespoons butter
4 tablespoons flour
1 cup milk
1/2 cup cream
salt
pepper
paprika
2 tablespoons sherry
1 dozen small raw oysters (or mussels)
1 cup cooked small shrimp

poach the fillets in court-bouillon and remove to a well buttered baking dish

melt the butter in a small saucepan, stir in the flour until well blended and slightly brown, then stir in 1/2 cup of the court-bouillon, 1 cup milk, and 1/2 cup cream. simmer until sauce is thick

add a little paprika, the sherry, and season to taste with salt and pepper

cover the fillets with the oysters and shrimp, pour on the sauce, glaze under the broiler until browned

(4 servings)

FILLETS OF SOLE VERMOUTH

4 fillets (about 2 1/2 pounds)
1/2 teaspoon salt
1 cup dry vermouth
1/4 cup fish stock
2 egg yolks
1 tablespoon heavy cream
pinch cayenne
1 cup butter

sprinkle the fillets with salt, roll up, fasten with toothpicks, and poach gently in the vermouth and stock for about 10 minutes or until fork-flaky. remove to an oven-proof serving dish and keep warm

reduce the cooking liquid by boiling to about 1/4 cup

place a small bowl into a pan containing a little simmering water. put in the egg yolks, cream, cayenne, and reduced liquid, and beat with whisk until thickened. whisk in the butter in small pieces until the sauce is creamy

pour the sauce over the fillets and glaze under the broiler for a couple of minutes or until sauce is golden

(4 servings)

FILLETS OF SOLE MORNAY

4 fillets (about 2 1/2 pounds)
1/2 cup fish fumet (see index)
mornay sauce (see index)
2 tablespoons butter
1/2 teaspoon salt
4 tablespoons grated parmesan or gruyere cheese

poach the fillets in enough fumet to half cover until flesh flakes when fork-tested

coat the bottom of an oven-proof serving dish with mornay sauce, drain the fillets, and place them on the sauce

dot the fillets with pieces of butter, cover with more of the mornay sauce, sprinkle with salt and grated cheese, and glaze under the broiler until golden

(4 servings)

FILLETS OF SOLE PROVENÇALE

2 pounds fillets
1/2 cup fumet (see index)
1 teaspoon salt
Provençale sauce (see index)
chopped parsley
8 small mushroom caps, lightly sautéed in butter

poach the fillets one or two at a time in the fumet until flesh flakes when fork-tested

transfer to a preheated serving platter and season with salt

cover the fillets with Provençale sauce, garnish with chopped parsley, and mushroom caps

(4 servings)

FILLETS OF SOLE MARINIÈRE

2 pounds fillets
1 cup clam broth
1 teaspoon salt
2 shallots, chopped
1 clove garlic, minced
2 teaspoons velouté
(see index)
1 egg yolk
1/2 cup butter
1 teaspoon chopped parsley

poach the fillets in the clam broth, transfer to an oven dish, season with salt, sprinkle with shallots and garlic

reduce the cooking liquid to half, thicken with velouté and egg yolk, and remove from the heat. stir in the butter and parsley and pour over the fillets

glaze quickly under the broiler

(4 servings)

FILLETS OF SOLE MEUNIÈRE

2 1/2 pounds fillets
1 teaspoon salt
1/2 teaspoon white pepper
flour
1/2 cup butter
2 tablespoons chopped parsley
1 lemon, sliced

dry the fillets well, season with salt and pepper, and sprinkle lightly with flour

melt the butter in a very hot heavy skillet and brown the fillets one or two at a time on both sides

serve garnished with chopped parsley and lemon slices

(4 servings)

FILLETS OF SOLE WITH SHRIMP

4 fillets (about 2 1/2 pounds)
1 cup dry white wine
4 mushrooms, sliced
8 medium raw shrimp, shelled
1/2 teaspoon salt
few grains cayenne
3 tablespoons butter
1 tablespoon flour
2 egg yolks mixed with 1/2 cup cream
2 teaspoons lemon juice
chopped fresh dill or parsley

place the fillets, mushrooms, shrimp, salt, and cayenne into a skillet with the wine, and simmer at low heat for about 10 minutes or until fish flakes and shrimp turns pink

carefully remove fillets to a serving platter, garnish with mushrooms and shrimp, and keep warm

melt the butter in a small saucepan, stir in the flour, cook for a few minutes, then stir in the egg-cream mixture

strain the skillet liquid and add to the saucepan, check for seasoning, stir in the lemon juice, and pour over the fish. garnish with chopped fresh dill

(4 servings)

FILLETS OF SOLE WITH OYSTERS

2 pounds fillets
1/2 cup butter
1 teaspoon lemon
1 teaspoon salt
1 dozen medium oysters
1 teaspoon
Worcestershire sauce
1/2 cup dry bread crumbs

pan-broil the fillets in butter and lemon juice until they flake when fork-tested, transfer to an oven dish, and season with salt

poach the oysters in their own liquid with Worcestershire until edges curl, transfer to the oven dish with the fillets, cover all with bread crumbs, moisten with the cooking liquid, and glaze under the broiler

(4 servings)

variations: cover the fillets and oysters with normandie sauce (see index) before glazing

FILLETS OF SOLE BONNE FEMME

2 pounds fillets
1 cup court-bouillon #1
(see index)
1 teaspoon salt
2 shallots, chopped
1 teaspoon chopped parsley
2 medium mushrooms,
minced
2 teaspoons velouté
(see index)

poach the fillets in the court-bouillon

transfer to an oven dish, season with salt, and sprinkle with shallots, parsley, and mushrooms

reduce the court-bouillon to half, thicken with velouté, pour over the fillets, and glaze under the broiler

(4 servings)

FILLETS OF SOLE DIEPPOISE

2 pounds fillets
fumet (see index)
1 1/2 dozen mussels
(shelled and bearded)
1 dozen small, fresh
shrimp, shelled
white wine sauce
(see index)

poach the fillets in the fumet until flesh flakes when fork-tested and remove to a heated platter

poach the mussels and shrimp in the same fumet, place around the fillets, and cover with white wine sauce

(4 servings)

FILLETS OF SOLE IN WHITE WINE

2 pounds fillets
1/2 cup fumet (see index)
1/2 cup dry white wine
1 teaspoon salt
1/2 teaspoon pepper
sauterne sauce or white
wine and egg sauce
(see index)
chopped watercress

poach the fillets in the fumet and wine until flesh is flaky when fork-tested

season with salt and pepper

remove to a heated serving platter, cover with sauce, and garnish with watercress

(4 servings)

FILLETS OF SOLE HUNGARIAN STYLE

3 tablespoons butter 1 onion, finely chopped 1 teaspoon paprika 4 tablespoons fumet (see index) 4 tablespoons dry white wine 1 tomato, peeled, seeded, and chopped 2 pounds fillets 4 tablespoons cream few drops lemon juice	sauté the onion and paprika in the butter without browning, add the fumet, wine, and tomato, and simmer for a few minutes fold the fillets and poach them one or two at a time in the liquid until flesh flakes when fork-tested remove fillets carefully to a heated serving dish reduce the poaching liquid until thickened, stir in the cream and lemon juice, and pour over the fillets (4 servings)

FILLETS OF SOLE AMBASSADRICE

top 4 poached fillets with cooked oysters and minced mushrooms and cover with sauce normandie* (4 servings)

FILLETS OF SOLE ANCIENNE

top 4 poached fillets with small onions and mushrooms that have been lightly cooked in butter. serve with fish velouté* (4 servings)

FILLETS OF SOLE ARGENTEUIL

top 4 poached fillets with cooked asparagus points and cover with sauterne sauce* (4 servings)

FILLETS OF SOLE COQUELIN

place 4 fillets into a baking dish, cover with chopped shallots, chopped mushrooms, *fines herbs* that have been simmered in white wine, and poach in a fumet. serve with fish velouté* (4 servings)

* (see index for sauces)

FILLETS OF SOLE GRAND DUC

top 4 fillets with thin slices of truffle, fold in two, cover with sauce mornay,* and brown under the grill. serve with asparagus points (4 servings)

FILLETS OF SOLE HONGROISE

top 4 poached fillets with fish velouté to which tomato purée and paprika have been added. dot with butter and place in oven for a few minutes (4 servings)

FILLETS OF SOLE MIRABEAU

using a heavy skillet, sauté 4 fillets in anchovy butter.* serve garnished with anchovy fillets and fresh tarragon (4 servings)

FILLETS OF SOLE NEWBURG

top 4 poached fillets with newburg sauce.* serve garnished with minced parsley (4 servings)

FILLETS OF SOLE ORIENTAL

top 4 poached fillets with curry sauce* and serve on a bed of rice (4 servings)

FILLETS OF SOLE PERSIAN

top 4 poached fillets with newburg sauce* seasoned with paprika and chopped pimientos, and serve with saffron rice or pilaf (4 servings)

FILLETS OF SOLE WALEWSKA

place 4 fillets into a baking dish, cover with raw truffles, sliced, lobster pieces that have been cooked in butter, and sauce mornay.* brown briefly under the grill (4 servings)

* (see index for sauces)

SQUID AND OCTOPUS

The squid has a long, slender gray body with a flat caudal fin at one end and ten short arms or tentacles with suction discs at the other.

A peculiarity of the fish is a brownish liquid which it emits to becloud waters when attacked. The liquid is used commercially to make sepia ink or paint, and gastronomically to make a sauce.

Averaging from 6 to 12 inches in length (the smaller they are the better they taste), squid are found in plentiful quantities along the Mediterranean shores where they are considered a delicacy and—to a lesser extent—along both coasts of the United States and in the Gulf region. Very large species have been discovered in mid-ocean depths.

Squid are available in many seafood markets in the United States, are bought mostly by the Spanish and Italians who serve them stuffed, sliced, fried, or stewed in their own black juices.

The octopus is a fish of another color (in fact, he can be almost any color he wants to be—even red—depending upon his mood). His body is soft and oval, he has a beak, large, human-like eyes, eight long arms or tentacles covered with suction discs, and moves about with great rapidity by jet propulsion.

Like squid, octopuses (or is it octopi?) abound in the warm waters of the Mediterranean Sea, but can also be found along the California coast and around Hawaii, where they are eaten raw (you skin the tentacles, cut them into slices). Frozen octopuses, imported from Spain, are frequently seen in Eastern markets. Gastronomically, the octopus is similar to the squid and is prepared in the same way.

STUFFED SQUID

4 squid (about 2 pounds)
2 cloves garlic, chopped
1 onion, finely chopped
2 tomatoes, finely chopped
3 tablespoons olive oil
2 tablespoons chopped
parsley
3 egg yolks
chunk of French bread
(fist size) soaked in milk
and squeezed dry
2 tablespoons water
1 onion, chopped
1 clove garlic, crushed
1 bay leaf
1 teaspoon salt
1/2 teaspoon pepper
2 tablespoons olive oil
glass dry white wine
glass water
dry bread crumbs
butter

clean the squid (see index), remove the ink sac, and discard. chop the tentacles finely

mix the chopped tentacles with the garlic, onion, tomatoes, and parsley, sauté gently for 2 minutes in a skillet

add the soaked bread, moisten with 2 tablespoons water, add the egg yolks, remove from the heat, and blend well

almost fill the squid bodies with this forcemeat, sew or skewer firmly, and place into a well oiled sauté pan

meanwhile, prepare a sauce by sautéeing onion, garlic, bay leaf, salt, and pepper in oil, and blending in flour. thin with water and wine, simmer for 15 minutes, and strain over the squid

sprinkle with bread crumbs, dot with butter, and brown in a preheated 300° oven. serve with the sauce poured over

(4 servings)

SQUID IN "INK"

2 pounds squid	cut off the heads, slit open the bellies, remove and discard the intestines
2 onions, chopped	
1 clove garlic, crushed	
1/2 cup oil	cut squid into pieces, save the "ink"
1/2 teaspoon salt	
pinch cayenne	gently sauté the onions and garlic in the oil, add the squid, salt, and cayenne, and then the "ink" and water
1/2 cup water	
	cover and simmer 2 hours. serve with crusty French bread (4 servings)

octopus can be used instead, but it's tougher to get in the United States and it's a lot tougher to eat

Don't be a slave to the recipe—improvise.

When making a roux, always stir the flour into the melted butter away from the heat. Add cream to achieve desired consistency. Blend with a wire whisk to avoid lumps.

SWORDFISH

One of the largest of the marine fish (weighing up to 500 pounds), swordfish, like halibut, is sold in the market almost exclusively as steaks. Richer and firmer than halibut, the meat sometimes tends to be oily.

SWORDFISH STEAK WITH MUSHROOMS

2 1/2 pounds swordfish steaks
1/2 cup flour
1 teaspoon salt
freshly ground pepper
pinch cayenne
pinch basil
2 tablespoons butter
3 slices raw bacon
1 cup fish stock
1/2 pound mushrooms, sliced

mix the flour, salt, pepper, cayenne, and basil, and sprinkle onto both sides of the steaks

place the steaks in a buttered baking dish, lay the bacon strips across, and pour over the fish stock

bake in a preheated 350° oven for half an hour, basting frequently

add mushrooms, return to the oven, and bake 15 minutes longer

baste again and serve

(4 servings)

alternate steaks: lingcod, cod

TERRAPIN AND TURTLES

Diamond Back Terrapin live along the marshy edges of gulfs, bays, and inlets of the Atlantic and Gulf of Mexico, and "Cooters," a freshwater species, are found in Southern waters.

Turtles are a freshwater animal, the most glamorous variety being the snapping turtle or snapper, from which the famous Philadelphia Snapper soup is made.

All varieties are sold live from time to time in specialty seafood markets. While I was researching this section of the book, I came upon a fish market on Ninth Avenue in New York City which displayed live snapping turtles. In fact, at that very moment a woman was busy buying one. Here, I thought, is my chance to learn something about how to prepare snapper.

"Pardon me," I said. "Would you mind telling me how you are going to go about killing and cooking that turtle?"

"Kill him?" she said. "I wouldn't kill him, I'm buying him as a pet."

The directions I finally dug up for killing and dressing terrapin and turtles may be found by consulting the index. I suspect that very few of my readers are going to undertake this gruesome task. Actually, turtle and terrapin meat are sometimes available frozen, and snapper soup can be had canned.

TERRAPIN À LA MARYLAND

once upon a time terrapin was almost as plentiful on the tables of Southern Maryland diners as oysters and crabs. not so any longer. I had to dig several generations back for the three recipes that follow which, by the way, I have not tested. with complete confidence in their authenticity and workability, however, I offer them to adventuresome cooks who might be able to get their hands on a couple of real live terrapin

---

TERRAPIN NO. 1

"Have two pots of boiling water, one for cleaning and one for cooking the terrapin. Drop the live terrapin in the boiling water for about 3 minutes and, with a towel, rub off the skin from the legs, clip off the toes and pull out the head and clean skin from same. After this, put in pot of boiling water and let boil until they feel soft to the touch. A 5-inch terrapin takes about 45 minutes to cook. After cooking, break the shell apart and let terrapin cool off sufficiently to handle. Then break the terrapin in joints, separating the meat from the bones and entrails. Save and wash the eggs. After having the meat and liver of the terrapin, add some of the stock in which you have cooked it.

To serve: Put the terrapin meat in a saucepan or chafing dish and cook with plenty of butter, a little pepper and salt. Cook about 10 minutes, then add the eggs and serve. (Add sherry, if desired) *Note*: I am told that a 5-inch terrapin should be cooked only 30 minutes and a 7-inch terrapin about 40 minutes, but you can always tell, because when a terrapin is cooked its shell begins to open and it should immediately be taken out of the water. A great deal of care should be taken in cleaning the legs and the neck and head of the terrapin with a rough cloth. When the terrapin is opened, the blood should be carefully saved and poured over the prepared terrapin in the jar when it is to be put away. Some people take out all of the entrails, but the proper way is to very carefully remove only the gall bladder and sandbag. The gall bladder should be completely taken out, even if you have to sacrifice a little of the liver in doing it. The meat of the terrapin itself should be separated from the bones, but only the large bones taken out. All the joint bones should be left in, but separate it out nearly as possible into pieces that will be convenient when eating."

W. L. Andrews
Baltimore
January 26, 1924

TERRAPIN NO. 2

"One large or 2 small terrapins put into boiling water for 10 minutes. Change the water and let boil half-hour or until done. Pull toenails out as a test. After partly cool, open, being careful not to break the sandbag (in the head) or the gallbag (in the liver). Put the terrapin in a saucepan with a little salt, if necessary, a pinch of dry mustard and a little cayenne pepper. Cover with water and let simmer slowly. Have yolks of hard-boiled eggs rubbed smoothly with 1/2 pound of butter and stir in slowly. Let cook a few minutes, then beat the yolks of 2 raw eggs and stir in very carefully. Do not let it boil, or it will curdle. After taking from the

fire, add a teacup of wine—Madeira or sherry—and a wineglass
of brandy. This can be re-heated by using a double boiler, without
curdling."

> Mrs. Barton Longacre Keen
> St. Anne's Parish
> Annapolis, Maryland
> 1937

TERRAPIN NO. 3

"Meat of 1 terrapin (everything but the skin, gall and outer shell)

1 tablespoon flour	6 tablespoons butter
2 hard-boiled eggs	1/4 cup sherry
1/2 cup of thick cream	

Rub the butter into the flour, put into a pan and add the terrapin. As soon as hot, add cream, the yokes of the eggs rubbed
smooth and the seasoning. Let it come to a boil, add wine and
serve immediately."

> Jeanette Cromwell
> Roland Park Garden Club
> 1935

SNAPPER STEW

1 onion, finely chopped
1 clove garlic, finely chopped
2 tablespoons butter
2 tablespoons flour
2 cups water
1 bay leaf
pinch thyme
1/2 teaspoon salt
1/2 teaspoon pepper
few grains cayenne
2 pounds snapping turtle meat, cut into 1-inch cubes
1/2 cup sherry or Madeira
2 teaspoons chopped fresh dill

in a heavy skillet, sauté the
onion and garlic in the butter
for a minute or so, stir in the
flour, then the water and seasonings. blend well

add the turtle meat, cover,
and simmer gently for half an
hour or until meat is tender

ten minutes before serving
pour in the wine. garnish with
fresh dill

(4 servings)

TROUT

Rainbow, steel-head, cut-throat, speckled, mountain, brook, brown—they're all trout. And they're all found in fast-moving fresh waters where there's lots of oxygen. Having no scales, few bones, and firm sweet flesh, all varieties, large or small, are regarded as a great culinary delicacy. So popular have trout become in recent years, that fish farms have been springing up all over the country to supply the ever-increasing demand, and frozen trout have become more and more available.

POACHED TROUT WITH SHALLOTS

4 brook trout, about 1/2 pound each

court-bouillon #1 (or dry white wine and salted water mixed 50-50)

3/4 cup chopped shallots (or scallions) mixed with 1/4 cup chopped chives

1 stick butter

3 tablespoons flour

2 cups milk

salt

pepper

cayenne

1 egg yolk

paprika

eviscerate the trout and remove the fins and tail (leave the heads on)

poach them gently for 3 minutes in enough court-bouillon to half cover them, turn, and cook 3 minutes longer

meanwhile, sauté the scallions and chives in the butter, sprinkle in the flour, and cook gently for 5 minutes. stir in the milk and cook for a few minutes longer, season to taste with salt, pepper, and cayenne. carefully stir in the egg yolk, but do not boil

place the trout on a warm serving platter, pour the sauce over them, sprinkle with paprika, and serve

(4 servings)

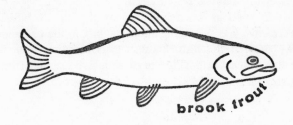

brook trout

RAINBOW TROUT EN PAPILLOTE

**4 rainbow trout, about
1 pound each, cleaned
but with heads intact
1 teaspoon salt
1/2 teaspoon white pepper
butter
2 tablespoons chopped
fresh mint
1/2 cup velouté sauce
(see index)**

season the fish inside and out with salt and pepper

cut parchment cooking paper or waxed paper into ovals larger than the fish, brush with butter, and fold vertically, then open again

place the trout onto the right half of each papillote, sprinkle with chopped mint, and cover with velouté sauce. fold left half of paper over and seal the edges by crimping them together

place the papillotes onto a greased cookie sheet and bake in a preheated 400° oven for half an hour

serve in the papillotes which will be puffed and brown

(4 servings)

almost any small fish can be prepared this way. experiment with the papillotes to make them attractive. inflate them by blowing into a soda straw inserted into the seam

TRUITES FARCIES (STUFFED TROUT)

we had this unforgettable dish at La Pyramide in Vienne, France, several months after the death of the great owner-chef, Fernand Point. Mme. Point was doing an excellent job of carrying on the tradition of this famous restaurant and I am sure the *truites* were every bit as good as when prepared by the master himself. the trout were alive and swimming about happily in the backyard tank when we ordered the dish, because discriminating French chefs believe that whenever possible trout should be served fresh from the water

2 small carrots, minced
4 small mushrooms, minced
2 small celery stalks, minced
1 truffle, minced (available in cans)
4 tablespoons butter
salt
pepper
3 tablespoons flour
3 egg yolks mixed with 1/2 cup milk
4 1/2-pound brook trout, cleaned but with heads intact
1 medium onion, minced
1 teaspoon thyme
1 1/2 cups fish stock
1/2 cup port wine
1/2 cup cream
2 tablespoons butter creamed with 2 tablespoons flour
8 cooked shrimp
8 cooked mushroom caps
1 lemon slice
parsley

cook the carrots, mushrooms, celery, and truffles in the butter for 10 minutes at low temperature. season to taste with salt and pepper, stir in the flour, and then egg-milk mixture. cook-stir until thick. remove and chill

stuff the trout with the vegetable mixture, skewer or sew, place into a buttered shallow casserole, and sprinkle with minced onion and thyme. add the fish stock and wine, cover with buttered paper, and bake in a preheated 350° oven for half an hour. remove to a preheated serving dish

strain the cooking liquid into a small saucepan, add the cream, the butter-flour roux, and cook, stirring until thickened. add a little port wine and pour the sauce over the fish. garnish each trout with 2 shrimp, 2 mushrooms, and truffle slices

serve with lemon slices and parsley

(4 delicious servings)

TUNA

Fresh tuna steak, appearing frequently in neighborhood fish stores, is rich, oily, and red in color. A little goes a long way. Smaller tuna, called albacore, have whiter, leaner flesh more suitable for serving fresh.

In cooking, apply almost any of the large fish recipes, such as kingfish, lingcod, halibut, swordfish . . .

TUNA STEAK ROYALE

1-inch thick fresh tuna steak (about 2 1/2 pounds)
1 teaspoon salt
freshly ground pepper
1/4 teaspoon paprika
pinch nutmeg
1/2 cup butter
1/2 cup chopped stuffed olives
2 tablespoons chopped parsley

wipe steak with paper napkin and cover both sides with a mixture of salt, pepper, paprika, and nutmeg

using a heavy skillet, pan broil the steak in butter about 5 minutes on each side or until flesh flakes with a fork. remove to a hot serving platter

toss the chopped olives into the skillet, sauté for a minute or so in the juices, and pour over the steak. garnish with chopped parsley and serve

(4 servings)

alternate steaks: black sea bass, king mackerel

WEAKFISH

Often called sea trout, this fish is definitely not related to the fresh-water fish of the same name. Averaging from 1 to 5 pounds, weakfish is sold in season whole, dressed, or filleted.

BAKED WEAKFISH, EGG SAUCE

1 weakfish (about 2 pounds), dressed, split, backbone removed
1 teaspoon salt
1/4 teaspoon pepper
1 onion, sliced
2 carrots, julienned
1/2 teaspoon chopped fresh dill
1/2 cup olive oil
2 egg yolks beaten with 2 tablespoons cream
paprika

cut the fish into 4 portions, place into a greased baking dish, season with salt and pepper, and cover with onions, carrots, dill, and olive oil

bake in a preheated 375° oven for half an hour or until fish flakes when fork-tested. transfer fish, onions, and carrots to a heated serving platter

place the baking dish over low heat, add the egg-cream mixture, and stir until thickened pour the sauce over the fish and dust with paprika

(4 servings)

croakers, closely related to weakfish, can be substituted

WHALE

Everybody knows that a whale is not a fish. But whale is seafood and, although only occasionally available in the market (corned, canned and—more rarely—frozen or fresh), it certainly rates mention in this kind of book.

There are many species of whales, differing in size and name—and presumably in the quality of their meat, but gastronomically only the calves, or young, are of value. At the present time, whale fanciers are more numerous among the Japanese, Eskimos, and Laplanders, but if whales don't become extinct first, the day might not be far away when all of us accept as everyday fare sizzling whale steaks, stews, pot roast, and the inevitable leftover favorite —whale hash.

For the present, if you find yourself with a chunk of whalemeat on hand, treat it as you would venison or beef—and if it's tough, marinate it.

THE WHELK

The whelk, or conch, is a large spiral-shelled, snail-like mollusk found along the beaches everywhere. It has a fleshy body and a broad foot upon which it crawls carrying its shell above.

Although not often eaten by Americans, the whelk shows up from time to time in New York, Boston, and San Francisco fish markets where it is bought and enjoyed by people of European extraction who find the meat sweet and delicious though, like abalone, a little rubbery.

WHITEBAIT

These are the tiny young of the common herring. They measure from 2 to 3 inches in length and are pale green and translucent. They have a subtle, delicate flavor and are available in the American market from April to November. You eat the whole fish—without cleaning it.

FRIED WHITEBAIT

1 pound whitebait
salt
white pepper
flour
deep fat for frying
1 lemon, quartered

wash the fish well and dry them thoroughly

sprinkle with salt and pepper and roll in flour. toss gently in a sieve to remove excess flour, taking care not to break

fry in 400° deep fat several at a time for about 2 minutes or until golden brown or sauté them in butter

drain and serve with lemon wedges

(4 servings)

WHITEFISH

Whitefish abound in the cold depths of the Great Lakes where they grow to an average weight of 2 pounds. One of the most popular of the large freshwater fish, its flesh is fat, firm, and succulent. Broil it, poach it, bake it, serve it plain, or with a sauce—or use it for making "gefilte fish."

WHITEFISH WITH HERB STUFFING

1 whitefish (about 2 pounds dressed)
1/2 teaspoon salt
1/4 teaspoon pepper
1/4 teaspoon paprika
herb stuffing (see index)
chopped fresh dill or parsley
1 lemon, sliced

wipe fish dry, blend seasonings, and sprinkle onto fish inside and out

stuff fish loosely, place into well greased baking pan, and bake uncovered in preheated 375° oven for 40 minutes or until flesh flakes when fork-tested

serve garnished with chopped fresh dill and lemon slices

(4 servings)

this fish is excellent with almost any kind of stuffing—mushroom, celery, salt pork herb (see index)

WHITEFISH WITH SAUTERNE SAUCE

2 1 1/2-pound whitefish, dressed, split, and boned
court-bouillon (see index)
1 clove garlic, split
sauterne sauce (see index)

poach the fish in the court-bouillon to which the garlic has been added

transfer to a preheated serving platter, and cover with the sauce and serve

(4 servings)

WHITING

This is a New England fish related to the cod and haddock. Averaging from 1 to 4 pounds in the market, whiting may be cooked whole or filleted. Most recipes for lean fish of comparable size would apply—especially those for cod and scrod.

WHITING À LA BERCY

3 pounds whiting, cleaned and with backbone removed
1 teaspoon salt
1/2 teaspoon pepper
1/2 teaspoon thyme
2 teaspoons chopped shallots
2 tablespoons melted butter
1/2 cup dry white wine
minced parsley

place fish into a buttered casserole, sprinkle with salt, pepper, thyme, and shallots. moisten with melted butter and wine and bake in a preheated 375° oven for half an hour or until fish is flaky when fork-tested. baste occasionally glaze under the broiler, sprinkle with minced parsley, and serve

(4 servings)

SEAFOOD SPECIALTIES

CAVIAR

without a doubt the top glamour appetizer the world over is caviar —especially the gray caviar made from the roe of the sturgeon family caught in the estuaries of rivers flowing into and around the Caspian Sea. the largest member of the family, the white sturgeon or beluga, produces the largest and best caviar, but it does not keep well and is not widely exported. caviar from the common sturgeon is smaller, but it keeps well and is shipped in vacuum tins

there is a small black caviar (usually artificially colored) made from the roe of fish other than sturgeon, and a red caviar, that comes from the roe of salmon. the flavor of these two is distinctively inferior to that of sturgeon caviar

serve caviar in its original tin (or in a glass bowl, if you wish), embedded in cracked ice. on the side, provide buttered toast or thin slices of pumpernickel or rye bread, chopped onion (or thin onion rings), chopped hard-cooked eggs (yolks and whites served separately), and sour cream or lemon wedges. keep caviar in the refrigerator but never in the freezer!

CEBICHE

most everybody knows that the Japanese and the Hawaiians—and most of the other Pacific people—take great delight in eating raw fish. actually, the fish they eat is not raw, but it isn't cooked either. It's marinated

I first met this "raw" fish in Acapulco, Mexico, where it is called *cebiche* and I can recommend it. we sat in bathing suits on the beach, protected from the hot sun by a thatched umbrella and consumed cebiche and good Mexican beer. later, we watched fishermen seining along the shores of Acapulco Bay for fat little silvery fish 5 or 6 inches long (the surf was thick with diving pelicans offering stiff competition), and I learned that these little fish were used principally in the preparation of cebiche

you can make cebiche with almost any lean white fish such as flounder, gray sole, or ocean perch

1 1/2 pounds fillet, cut into 1-inch squares
1 tablespoon ground dry red chili (or a few dashes Tabasco sauce)
2 onions, thinly sliced
1 clove garlic, finely chopped
1 teaspoon salt
1 tablespoon cracked peppercorns
1 cup lime juice
1 cup lemon juice

place all the ingredients into a glass, enamel, or stainless steel dish, mix well, and make certain that the fish is completely covered with the marinade

place in the refrigerator for 3 or 4 hours until fish is white and opaque

serve with toothpicks

(4 to 6 servings)

CLAMS CASINO

here is a delicious first cousin of Oysters Rockefeller

6 slices bacon
1/2 cup minced shallots (or scallions)
1/4 cup minced green pepper
1/4 cup minced celery
few drops Worcestershire sauce
few drops Tabasco sauce
24 medium clams on the half shell

cook the bacon until crisp. drain, dry, crumble, and set aside

to the bacon fat add the shallots, minced pepper, celery, Worcestershire and Tabasco. cool for a minute or two

spoon this sauce over the half-shell clams, top with crumbled bacon, and bake in a pre-heated 450° oven until the sauce bubbles (4 or 5 minutes) serve at once

(4 servings as a main dish, 8 as an appetizer)

CODFISH CAKES

1/2 pound salt cod, cut into pieces and soaked in cold water overnight
1 cup mashed potatoes
2 eggs
flour
cooking fat

cover the codfish pieces with water, bring to a boil, discard the water, and repeat. taste the water and if salty, continue changing until saltiness disappears and fish flakes when fork-tested

flake the fish and mix with the potatoes and eggs

form into 8 cakes, roll in flour, and fry in deep fat at 370° until golden

(4 servings)

COD CHEEKS AND TONGUES MADRILÈNE

here's one that will make your guests take notice. all you have to do is get hold of a batch of cod cheeks and tongues and toss them into a skillet with a little very hot olive oil containing a clove of garlic. after a minute or so you cover the tongues with vinegar and season with thyme, powdered bay leaf, and a little hot Spanish pepper. after about 10 minutes you sprinkle with chopped fennel, leave them to cool in their own juices, and serve cold on toothpicks

COQUILLES ST. JACQUES

coquilles are little fireproof dishes made in the shape of a scallop shell into which various preparations are put and browned in the oven

to make Coquilles St. Jacques, mix chopped scallops (or lobster, shrimp, or crabmeat) with velouté sauce (see index), season with Worcestershire, sherry, or brandy, and spoon into the shells. sprinkle with grated Parmesan cheese and/or bread crumbs and brown in a hot oven. serve hot. two of these per guest as appetizers—more as a main lunch course

ELVERS

These are the young of the European eel. Spawned in the depths of the western Atlantic, they appear seasonally in European rivers after an incredible trip of two years. Complete little eels, only two inches long, and nearly transparent in color, elvers are a great treat to many European gourmets.

I encountered elvers at the Jockey Club in Madrid where they were served as a very special first course. I didn't order them, but my wife did and I was invited to taste. Looking a lot like linguine, they had been prepared with a delicate garlic-butter sauce, and had a rich, subtle flavor.

FRIED ELVERS

since elvers are unavailable in the American market, it seems scarcely appropriate to go into the details of cooking them. but, just in case you find yourself in Europe and find yourself with a couple of pounds of elvers on hand, here's how you can cook up a dish you're not likely to forget for a long time. there's just one problem—elvers have a way of sticking together as you fry them, and coming out in a gelatinous mass. to avoid this, you should first wash the little beasts well and then dry them thoroughly. next you dust them lightly but completely with flour, taking care that there isn't an excess of flour to create little lumps of paste, then you season them lightly with salt. and, finally you fry them in boiling oil containing a split clove of garlic

if the job is done right, each elver will come out separate, crisp, and delicious. serve with wedges of lemon

---

FISH MOUSSE

2 cups fish forcemeat (pike, whiting, carp, etc.) (see index)
2 tablespoons butter
garnish
sauce

butter a round mold or a mold with a hole in the middle and fill almost to the top with fish mousse

set the mold into a pan of hot water and bake in a preheated 375° oven for about half an hour

remove from heat, let stand for a few minutes, and turn out onto a heated platter

garnish as desired and spoon on appropriate sauce

(4 to 6 servings)

SOME GARNISHES FOR FISH MOUSSE

shelled mussels cooked in white wine combined with mushrooms sautéed in butter (dieppoise)

poached oysters and/or steamed shrimp combined with mushrooms sautéed in butter (normandie)

chopped cooked shrimp, chopped mushrooms, and chopped truffles blended into velouté sauce (see index)

shrimp steamed or cooked in white wine

mussels steamed or cooked in white wine

SOME SAUCES FOR FISH MOUSSE

(the sauce and garnish should be compatible)

béchamel, cream maître d'hôtel, curry, shrimp, normandie, ravigote, white wine (see index)

FROG

Although frogs spend most of their adult years on land, they were born in water and so rate classification as seafood. They definitely are not meat.

Long a favorite food among the French, they are cultivated in great quantities in special ponds throughout the country. In recent years, they have been grown and marketed in the United States, although they are in short supply.

Only the plump hind legs, detached from the body in pairs and skinned, are of gastronomic value. When soaked in several changes of very cold water, the flesh whitens and swells. Usually three pairs per serving are enough.

FROGS' LEGS PROVENÇALE

season the frogs' legs, dip them lightly in flour, and sauté in butter containing a little crushed garlic and chopped parsley. Serve with lemon wedges

FROGS' LEGS À L'ANGLAISE

season the frogs' legs, flour them and dip them in egg and bread crumbs. sauté in butter and serve with maître d'hôtel butter (see index)

FROGS' LEGS À LA HORSHER

here is a recipe Otto Horsher, himself, gave me when I visited his restaurant in Madrid. I liked frogs' legs prepared this way and so did my wife. try it—you'll see

dip the frogs' legs in milk, then sprinkle with salt, a little cayenne pepper, and flour. sauté in butter containing a little garlic and a cup of mushroom caps until legs and mushrooms are golden brown. add 4 tablespoons dry white wine and 4 tablespoons dry sherry and simmer gently for about 10 minutes. serve garnished with minced parsley and paprika

GEFILTE FISH

3 pounds of fresh fish (whitefish, carp, mullet, pike—2 or more varieties)
3 onions, sliced
2 carrots, sliced
1 teaspoon salt
1/2 teaspoon pepper
2 cups water
3 onions, chopped
1 tablespoon matzo meal or 2 slices dry white bread
2 eggs
1 tablespoon sugar
1 teaspoon salt
1/2 teaspoon pepper
water

remove the heads, bones, and skin from the fish, cook with the onions, carrots, salt, and pepper in 2 cups water for an hour. strain and keep the stock

meanwhile put the fish flesh (no bones, please) into a blender with the chopped onions, matzo meal, eggs, sugar, salt, and pepper. blend well, moistening with water as needed

form into marble-sized balls, drop into the simmering stock, cover, and cook for 2 hours

serve cold with freshly made horseradish

(8 servings)

variation: instead of simmering the fish balls in stock, fry them in hot olive oil until golden, and serve hot or cold

GRAVLAX

this is a sort of Scandinavian version of *cebiche*. salmon is used instead of flatfish and the curing process is managed with salt instead of lime juice. Michael Field, who operates a famous cooking school in New York City, and writes famous cookbooks, makes it this way:

2 pounds fresh salmon, sliced lengthwise (the center cut is best), cleaned, boned, scaled, and cut in half lengthwise

1 bunch fresh dill

1/4 cup salt (coarse salt is best)

1/4 cup sugar

1 tablespoon cracked peppercorns

place half of the fish, skin side down into a glass, stainless steel, or enamel dish, cover with dill, sprinkle with salt, sugar, and peppercorns

place the other half of the fish on top, skin side up, cover with aluminum foil, and place weights on top

place in the refrigerator for 2 to 3 days, turning the fish and basting with the liquid that accumulates every 12 hours

remove the fish slices from the marinade, scrape off the seasonings, and dry with a paper towel

place on a carving board, skin side down, and slice thinly on the diagonal, removing each slice from the skin

serve iced with mustard sauce (see index)

(4 to 6 servings)

KIPPERS, BLOATERS, AND FINNAN HADDIE

A kipper is a herring that has been kippered. And how do you kipper a herring? First, you catch him, then you split him open, eviscerate him, salt him, and finally you smoke him. The end product is a fish that will keep for months and months without benefit of refrigeration.

The process was developed ages ago by herring fishermen off the coast of the British Isles who stayed at sea for many days. The fish are salted on board immediately after the catch to prevent spoilage and then smoked later when brought ashore.

Herring caught close enough to the coast to be brought in and cured while still fresh are called bloaters. Both fish are highly regarded by the British as breakfast dishes. Most of those available in the American market are dried and in tins.

New England fishermen apply this same treatment to their haddock catches and produce a delicious, sweet-tasting, but smelly fish which is called finnan haddie after (or so they say) the town of Findon in Scotland.

These salted and smoked fish (cod, too) taste better when soaked overnight before cooking.

PAN-FRIED BLOATERS

4 bloaters
2 eggs, well beaten
1/2 cup grated cheddar cheese
1/2 cup butter
chopped parsley

soak, skin, remove heads, tails, and bones of the bloaters

dip them into the beaten eggs, sprinkle on both sides with grated cheese, then flour, and fry them in butter at moderate temperature so that the butter does not smoke. 2 minutes on each side should do it

serve sprinkled with cheese and parsley

(4 servings)

FINNAN HADDIE IN MILK

cover the fish with milk, season to taste with salt and pepper, and cook, covered, for half an hour. serve dotted with butter

SALT COD PROVENÇALE

1 1/2 pounds salt cod fillets
1 bay leaf
1/2 teaspoon thyme
1/2 teaspoon chopped parsley
2 cloves garlic, chopped
3 shallots, chopped
2 tomatoes, skinned, seeded, and squeezed dry
salt
pepper
1/2 cup melted butter
1/2 cup olive oil
dijonnaise sauce (see index)

soak the cod fillets overnight, changing the water several times. drain

put the fillets into a skillet with the bay leaf, thyme, and parsley. cover with water and bring to a boil

remove from the heat, allow to stand in the liquid for 20 minutes. remove and drain

mix the garlic, shallots, and tomatoes, season with salt and pepper, and place half of this mixture in the bottom of a shallow baking dish. add the cod fillets and cover with the remaining mixture

sprinkle with butter and olive oil, bake in a preheated 375° oven for half an hour and serve with dijonnaise sauce

(4 servings)

OYSTERS ROCKEFELLER

every chef has his own idea of preparing this superb dish, so vary this recipe to suit yourself

1 cup melted butter
1/4 cup minced shallots (or scallions)
1/4 cup minced celery
1/4 cup minced parsley
1 cup minced watercress (or spinach)
1 clove garlic, minced
1/2 teaspoon dried chervil
1/2 teaspoon dried tarragon
1/4 cup soft bread crumbs
few drops Worcestershire sauce
few drops Tabasco sauce
1/2 teaspoon salt
2 tablespoons Pernod (if you like licorice flavor)
24 medium oysters on the half shell

mix all the ingredients (except the oysters) together in a blender, or grind them in a mortar

make a bed of damp rock salt in a shallow baking dish, arrange the half-shell oysters on the salt, and place a spoonful of the sauce on each

bake in a preheated 450° oven until sauce bubbles (4 or 5 minutes) serve at once

(4 servings as a main dish, 8 as an appetizer)

SEAFOOD PAELLA

paella, the national rice dish of Spain, is served everywhere throughout the country (and in Mexico, too). the ingredients used depend upon what kind of food is on hand. southern Spaniards say they invented the dish (it's named for the two-handled iron frying pan used in its preparation) and that Paella Valenciana is the only kind fit to eat

in fishing villages, paella is made without the customary chicken and sausages used further inland. a true seafood dish, it's made with whatever ingredients the sea gives forth at the time. in the following recipe feel free to substitute whatever seafood you have on hand, but remember that shellfish takes a very short time to cook and should go in last. control the consistency of the paella with the stock—it should be neither liquid nor dry, but firm

1/4 pound salt pork, cut into small cubes
1/2 cup olive oil
1 onion, chopped
2 cloves garlic, chopped
2 green peppers, chopped
1 teaspoon oregano
1/2 teaspoon coriander
1/2 teaspoon saffron
4 cups fish stock (see index)
2 cups raw rice
2 tomatoes, peeled, seeded, and squeezed dry
3 lobster tails, cut into pieces, shells discarded
2 or 3 baby squid, cleaned and cut into pieces
1 pound raw shrimp, deveined and shelled, but with tails intact
2 dried clams or mussels, scrubbed

using a large skillet or paella pan, render the pork. add the oil, onion, garlic, peppers, and seasonings. sauté gently for a few minutes

now pour in the stock, add the raw rice, cook for 5 minutes, and add the tomatoes. stir well to coat the rice with oil

cook the clams or mussels separately, and add them and the rest of the seafood to the paella, cover, and cook for 5 minutes longer. check the consistency and serve from the pan

(6 servings)

FISH ROE

All female fish produce roe—those little eggs encased in a thin membrane—but only that of certain species is considered commercially valuable. The roe of the sturgeon and of the salmon are marinated in salt and marketed as caviar, but many others are sold fresh, frozen, smoked, or canned. Included among these is the roe of the cod, carp, alewife, whitefish, mullet, herring, and shad. Most popular of all is shad roe. Each spring the shad migrate up the rivers of the East coast—the rivers of South Carolina, Virginia, Maryland, Delaware, and New York—to deposit their eggs for hatching. And each spring, to the delight of shad roe fanciers, great quantities are intercepted and their eggs are deposited instead on dining-room tables.

SHAD ROE WITH BACON

place the roe in a skillet with a little water, add a teaspoon of salt and a tablespoon of vinegar. cover and simmer gently for 5 minutes. drain, sprinkle with salt, pepper, and flour, and pan broil in bacon fat until golden. serve with bacon strips

you don't absolutely have to cook the roe in water, but the parboiling keeps the little eggs from exploding all over the place

vary the recipe by dipping the roe in beaten egg and cracker crumbs before cooking. And substitute any kind of roe you desire

---

SNAILS AND PERIWINKLES

snails are neither fish nor flesh, but for some reason are usually included among the seafood—they will be so included in this book

although you can find all kinds of snails in all kinds of places, the edible varieties are cultivated only in France, where they are grown on farms, fattened, and sent to the markets alive. before cooking they must be deprived of food for a specified period of time to avoid the risk of their eating foods poisonous to people, but harmless to themselves

snails are available in this country in cans, complete with shells to stuff them into, and directions for doing it

periwinkles are little snails of the sea, can be found along most the beaches of the United States, and in specialty seafood markets. unlike land snails, they're clean and do not require starving before cooking. you heat them a little in salted water. the sealing membrane breaks and the little animals retreat further into their shells. all you have to do is coax them out with a toothpick, simmer them a little in salted water and prepare them like snails

SNAILS PROVENÇAL

remove the snails from the can, stuff them into the shells (which you have prescrubbed), plug up the opening with snail butter, and bake them in a preheated 450° oven for 10 minutes

and here's how you make snail butter: cream 1/4 cup butter at room temperature with a clove crushed garlic, 1/4 cup minced parsley, a little salt, and freshly ground pepper. you'll have enough to plug 3 dozen snails, appetizers for 8—main course for 3

for the regular snail eaters, special snail equipment is available —dishes called *escargotières,* constructed with depressions to prevent the animals from rolling over and losing their juices, special snail pincers, and special snail forks

TRUITE AU BLEU

this is an unusual and superb dish, unusual because it's a vivid blue in color, and superb because the flavor is so fresh and delicate. the secret is that only freshly caught trout can be used

but it's not unusual to find blue trout in the restaurants of the Burgundy country of France, since so many of them have their own trout ponds where the fish swim about and wait for you to order them

I did . . . and here's what the chef did (I know, because I watched him): he dipped the trout, a frisky 9-inch beauty, from the pond with a net, broke its neck, and quickly deviscerated it. next, without washing or scaling it, he covered the fish (whole) with a wine court-bouillon (pre-prepared) and poached it for 4 or 5 minutes. he then brushed the now blue fish with melted sweet butter, sprinkled it with minced fresh parsley, and it was mine

WHITEBAIT AND OYSTER CRABS

this has long been a famous dish at the Hotel Barclay in Philadelphia. but you can find it on the menu only when both of the ingredients are in season. the whitebait and oyster crabs (these are the little pink crabs, fingernail-size, that live with oysters, sharing the hospitality of their shells and food) are carefully patted dry with a napkin, dusted lightly with rice flour and pan-fried in peanut oil and butter. they're served simply with chopped parsley and lemon

SCALLOPS IN THE RAW

marinate for 2 hours, 1/2 pound bay scallops (or quartered sea scallops) in enough fresh lime juice to cover. the citric acid will "cook" the scallops. drain and add 2 tablespoons chopped chives or scallions, 1 tablespoon chopped parsley, 4 tablespoons olive oil, and salt and pepper to taste. mix well, chill, and serve raw on toothpicks (4 servings)

COURTS-BOUILLONS, STOCKS, AND FUMETS

These are the liquids so necessary to the conscientious seafood cook in preparing superior sauces and soups, and for poaching fillets. Prepared in advance, and set aside in the refrigerator, they will save time and effort with many of the recipes in this book.

A court-bouillon is simply a prepared aromatic liquid usually composed of water, wine, or vinegar, and certain vegetable essences, seasonings, and spices. Fish fillets take on an added mysterious succulence when poached in a court-bouillon.

Here are five good courts-bouillons. When you study them you will see how easy it might be to compose your own mixture.

COURT-BOUILLON #1

1 quart water	put all the ingredients into a large pot, cover, and simmer for half an hour
1 quart dry white wine	
2 onions, thinly sliced	
1 bay leaf	strain and set aside until ready to use
pinch thyme	
few sprigs parsley	excellent for poaching fish
1/2 teaspoon peppercorns	(yields 1 1/2 quarts)
2 teaspoons salt	

COURT-BOUILLON #2

1 quart water	put all the ingredients into a large pot, cover, and simmer for half an hour
1 quart dry red wine	
1 onion, thinly sliced	
1 carrot, thinly sliced	strain and set aside until ready to use
1 stalk celery, chopped	
1 bay leaf	excellent for fish stews, and for cooking large fish such as trout or carp
pinch thyme	
few sprigs parsley	
1/2 teaspoon peppercorns	(yields 1 1/2 quarts)
2 teaspoons salt	

COURT-BOUILLON #3

1 quart water	put all the ingredients into a large pot, cover, and bring to a boil over low heat
1 quart milk	
1 bay leaf	
pinch thyme	strain and use for cooking finnan haddie
few sprigs parsley	
1/2 teaspoon peppercorns	(yields 1 1/2 quarts)

COURT-BOUILLON #4

2 tablespoons butter	melt the butter and sauté the vegetables for 5 minutes or until golden
1 onion, chopped	
1 carrot, chopped	
2 stalks celery, chopped	strain and set aside until ready to use in boiling or poaching fish like trout or flatfish. for shellfish, leave out the vinegar
2 quarts water	
2 tablespoons vinegar	
1 bay leaf	
few sprigs parsley	(yields 2 quarts)
1/2 teaspoon peppercorns	

COURT-BOUILLON #5

1/4 pound butter
1 carrot, chopped
2 stalks celery, chopped
1 onion, chopped
1 quart water
1 quart cider (or dry white wine)
1 bay leaf
pinch thyme
2 sprigs parsley
2 teaspoons salt
1/2 teaspoon peppercorns

melt the butter and sauté the vegetables for 5 minutes or until golden

add the water, cider, and seasonings. cover and cook for half an hour

strain and set aside until ready for use

(yields 2 quarts)

FISH STOCK

Fish stock is a broth made by simmering fish bones and trimmings (heads, tails, etc. . . .) in water and/or wine with or without the addition of various herbs and aromatics. A good stock is indispensable in the preparation of superior fish sauces, soups, and bouillabaisses—and it comes in handy as a moistener for baking and broiling lean fish.

STOCK #1

2 pounds fish trimmings (heads, bones, tails)
1 onion, thinly sliced
6 sprigs parsley
1 teaspoon lemon juice
1 cup dry white wine
2 quarts cold water
1/2 teaspoon peppercorns

put all the ingredients into a large soup kettle and bring to a boil

cut the heat, cover, and simmer for half an hour or so

strain and set aside

(yields 2 quarts)

STOCK #2, #3, #4, #5, #6

2 pounds fish trimmings (heads, bones, tails) **2 quarts of one of the courts-bouillons**	put the ingredients into a large pot, cover, and simmer for half an hour or so strain and set aside (yields 2 quarts)

FISH FUMET

A fumet is a concentrate made by reducing wine-based fish stock. *Cordon bleu* cooks lean heavily on fumets when preparing fish sauces and other sophisticated dishes. You, too, can give your seafood cooking extra richness with the use of a good fumet. Keep one on hand in the refrigerator.

2 quarts fish stock that has been made with wine (or add a quart of wine to a quart of stock made without wine)	put into an uncovered pot and simmer down to half the quantity set aside until ready to use (yields 1 quart)

SAUCES

Sauces are a sort of liquid seasoning for food. Especially important in sophisticated cooking, they often make the difference between an ordinary dish and a very special one.

The kitchen staffs of top hotels and restaurants invariably include a saucier whose sole role is to prepare the sauces that grace the various menu items. I watched a famous saucier at work in the kitchen of the old Savoy Plaza Hotel in New York. With infinite care to details, he blended ingredients little by little, tasting frequently as he added each, and during the cooking process itself, until he arrived at the flavor and consistency he was looking for.

It has been estimated that there are more than two hundred recipes for sauces in European and American cooking, thick and thin, brown and white, hot and cold, meat-based and fish-based. This book will cover the most important and most useful of the fish sauces, including some cold sauces for cocktails, canapés and cold entrées, as well as the more popular hot sauces.

BÉCHAMEL (BASIC WHITE SAUCE)

melt 4 tablespoons butter in a heavy saucepan and stir in 4 table-spoons flour, 1/2 teaspoon salt, and a pinch white pepper. keep the heat low or the flour will brown. slowly stir in 2 cups milk (or 1 cup milk and 1 cup cream) until the sauce is smooth and creamy (yields 1 to 1 1/2 cups)

there are numerous variations of this basic white sauce. some recipes call for the addition of such herbs and spices as chives, dill, cloves, parsley, and mace. some combine milk or cream with chicken stock. here are a few:

CELERY SAUCE

to basic white sauce add 1/2 cup finely chopped celery that has been cooked in water for 5 minutes

CURRY SAUCE

to basic white sauce add 1 teaspoon curry powder

EGG SAUCE

to basic white sauce add 3 hard-cooked eggs, finely chopped

HERB SAUCE

to basic white sauce add 1 tablespoon chopped fresh herbs (or 1/2 tablespoon dried herbs) such as parsley, chives, dill, etc. . . . .

MORNAY SAUCE

to basic white sauce add 1/2 cup grated Gruyere cheese and/or Parmesan cheese. just before serving, stir in an egg yolk, lightly beaten

MUSHROOM SAUCE

to basic white sauce add 1/2 cup finely chopped cooked mushrooms

MAYONNAISE

in addition to serving as a good all-purpose egg sauce for cold dishes, mayonnaise is the basis for a great many other cold sauces. although the store-bought kind will satisfy in a pinch, there's nothing like good homemade mayonnaise—and if you'll follow the rules, it's really not hard to make. just a word of caution: mayonnaise made with olive oil is more likely to separate out than that made with vegetable oil. if separation takes place, put an egg yolk into a bowl and gradually beat the mayonnaise into it

put 3 egg yolks into a bowl, season with a teaspoon salt, a pinch of white pepper, and add a few drops of lemon juice or vinegar. mix lightly with a whisk. now add 2 1/2 cups olive oil (or a good vegetable oil) drop by drop at first, then in a thin trickle, beating constantly with the whisk. thin down the consistency from time to time by adding a few drops of lemon juice or vinegar. when the sauce is finished, beat in 1 or 2 tablespoons boiling water to prevent curdling
(yields 3 cups)

ANCHOVY MAYONNAISE

follow the recipe for mayonnaise and mix 2 teaspoons anchovy paste into the beaten egg before adding the oil
(yields 3 cups)

HERB MAYONNAISE

follow the recipe for mayonnaise and mix 2 teaspoons *fines herbes*
(chopped chives, parsley, chervil, and tarragon) into the beaten
egg before adding the oil
(yields 3 cups)

SAUCE INDIENNE

follow the recipe for mayonnaise and mix 1/4 teaspoon curry
powder and 2 teaspoons chopped chives into the beaten egg before adding the oil
(yields 3 cups)

MUSTARD MAYONNAISE

follow the recipe for mayonnaise and mix 2 teaspoons dry mustard
into the beaten egg before adding the oil
(yields 3 cups)

TOMATO MAYONNAISE

follow the recipe for mayonnaise and mix a tablespoon tomato
purée into the beaten egg before adding the oil
(yields 3 cups)

GREEN MAYONNAISE (SAUCE VERTE)

make a purée of green herbs (spinach, watercress, parsley, tarragon) by blanching, cooling, and grinding in a mortar. mix with
2 1/2 cups mayonnaise
(yields 3 cups)

ANCHOVY BUTTER SAUCE

grind in a mortar, 10 anchovy fillets with 1/2 pound sweet butter and the yolks of 3 hard-cooked eggs. to this mixture add enough vinaigrette sauce (see index) to reach the desired consistency

BÉARNAISE SAUCE

add 1 teaspoon finely chopped parsley and 1 teaspoon finely chopped fresh tarragon (or a tablespoon tarragon vinegar) to Hollandaise

BEURRE NOIR

melt 1/2 cup butter in a small pan and cook over low heat until dark brown. add 1 teaspoon lemon juice and season to taste. use at once
(perform the above operation in the pan used for frying fish, using some of the remaining fat)

BURGUNDY SAUCE

in the top section of a double boiler, blend together 1 cup velouté sauce (see index) and 1 cup burgundy wine
(or substitute a dry claret, Chianti, or sweet vermouth)

DRAWN BUTTER

in the top section of a double boiler, blend together 2 tablespoons melted butter, 2 tablespoons flour, 1/2 teaspoon salt, and a little pepper. add, stirring, 1 cup fish stock or 1 cup hot water, teaspoon lemon juice, and 2 additional tablespoons butter
(for caper sauce, add 1 tablespoon capers to the above)
(yields 1 cup)

CHAMPAGNE SAUCE

in the top section of a double boiler, blend together 1 cup velouté sauce and 1 cup champagne. season with a little white pepper, a pinch mace, and 1/2 teaspoon sugar
(or substitute sauterne, Rhine wine, or dry vermouth)

COCKTAIL SAUCE

blend together 1 cup catsup, 1 tablespoon tarragon vinegar, 1 tablespoon prepared horseradish, 1 tablespoon very finely chopped onion, 1 teaspoon Worcestershire sauce, and 4 drops Tabasco sauce. season with a little salt and chill
(yields 1 1/2 cups)

DIJONNAISE SAUCE

using a mortar, grind the yolks of 4 hard-cooked eggs and 4 teaspoons Dijon mustard. season with salt and pepper and beat with a whisk while adding 2 1/2 cups olive oil, drop by drop, and 1 tablespoon lemon juice as in making mayonnaise
(yields 3 cups)

GERMAINE SAUCE

blend together 1 1/2 cups mayonnaise, 1 teaspoon lemon juice, 3 tablespoons catsup, 4 tablespoons heavy cream, 1 tablespoon brandy, a pinch salt, and a pinch white pepper
(yields 2 cups)

HOLLANDAISE SAUCE

in the top section of a double boiler, beat 3 egg yolks with a whisk or wooden spoon until smooth. add 2 tablespoons lemon juice or vinegar, 1/2 cup melted butter, 3 tablespoons hot water, a

pinch salt, and a few grains cayenne. continue beating until sauce thickens (about 5 minutes). remove from the heat—sauce will continue to thicken
(yields 1 cup)

HORSERADISH SAUCE

beat together 4 tablespoons grated horseradish, 2 egg yolks, and a little salt. beat egg whites until stiff, beat 1 pint heavy cream until stiff and blend the two. add the horseradish mixture and the juice of 1/2 lemon. mix and chill
(yields 2 cups)

HORSERADISH MARMALADE

blend 2 parts orange marmalade with 1 part prepared horseradish. add a few drops Worcestershire and thin to desired consistency with orange juice or water

SAUCE MAÎTRE D'HÔTEL

melt 1/2 cup butter in a small pan over low heat and stir in 2 tablespoons chopped parsley, 1 teaspoon chopped fresh tarragon (use half the quantity if dried), 1/2 teaspoon salt, and a little pepper. beat in, drop by drop, 1 tablespoon lemon juice. use at once
(to make maître d'hôtel cream sauce, mix the above with 1 cup velouté sauce)
yields 1/2 cup

NEWBURG SAUCE

in the top section of a double boiler, melt 2 tablespoons butter and stir in 2 tablespoons flour, a little dry mustard, cayenne, salt, and pepper. blend well for 2 minutes and gradually stir in 2 cups

light cream, then 2 well-beaten egg yolks, 1 tablespoon sherry, and 1 tablespoon brandy
(yields 2 1/2 cups)

SAUCE NORMANDIE

melt 3 tablespoons butter and stir in 3 tablespoons flour. cook for a few minutes, add 1 cup fish stock, and stir until the sauce thickens. season to taste with salt and pepper and stir in 1/2 pint heavy cream previously combined with 2 egg yolks. squeeze in a little lemon juice, stir, and serve at once—great for any kind of hot seafood
(yields 1 1/2 cups)

SAUCE PROVENÇALE

peel, squeeze out the seeds, and coarsely chop 6 tomatoes. season with salt and pepper and cook for half an hour in hot oil with a clove of crushed garlic, a pinch sugar, and 1 teaspoon chopped parsley

SAUCE RAVIGOTE

melt 2 tablespoons butter, add 4 minced shallots, and sauté about 10 minutes or until golden. add 1/2 teaspoon dry mustard, 1 cup dry sauterne, 1/2 teaspoon sugar, 2 tablespoons tomato paste, and salt to taste. cover and simmer gently for 20 minutes
(yields 4 servings)

SAUCE RÉMOULADE

mix 3 tablespoons chopped chives, 3 tablespoons chopped parsley, 1 teaspoon lemon juice, and a little Dijon mustard into 1 cup mayonnaise
(yields 1 1/2 cups)

SAUTERNE SAUCE

heat 1 cup dry sauterne in the top section of a double boiler for a few minutes. beat together 4 egg yolks, 2 teaspoons sugar, teaspoon vinegar, and stir this mixture gradually into the wine. continue stirring until sauce is thick
(yields 4 servings)

SHRIMP (OR LOBSTER) SAUCE

melt 2 tablespoons butter in the top section of a double boiler, stir in 1/2 teaspoon salt, a little white pepper, and 1/4 teaspoon paprika. blend 2 tablespoons flour and 1 cup milk until smooth and add to the melted butter. stir until thick and add 1 cup finely chopped, cooked shrimp (or lobster). check seasoning
(yields 4 servings)

TARTAR SAUCE

blend together 3/4 cup mayonnaise, 1 teaspoon finely chopped shallots or onion, 1 teaspoon finely chopped sweet pickles, 1 teaspoon finely chopped stuffed olives, and 1 teaspoon finely chopped parsley
(yields 1 cup)

VELOUTÉ SAUCE

velouté is the basis for many famous sauces and is a must in any cook's repertoire. Since this book concerns itself only with seafood, only fish velouté will be considered
melt 4 tablespoons butter in a heavy saucepan and stir in 4 tablespoons flour, 1/2 teaspoon salt and a pinch white pepper. blend well, keeping the heat low and then slowly stir in 2 cups fish fumet. simmer for 15 minutes and skim the scum. add 1 cup cream and stir until thick and smooth
(yields 2 cups)

SAUCE VINAIGRETTE (French Dressing)

dissolve 1/2 teaspoon salt in 4 tablespoons vinegar, then stir in 4 tablespoons oil and a little freshly ground pepper. use any oil (mild olive oil is best) and any vinegar (wine vinegar is best) but always use them in 50–50 proportions

this is the pure vinaigrette. you can vary it by adding any or all of the following: celery seed, garlic, cayenne, Worcestershire sauce, dill, thyme, sugar, etc. . . .

WHITE WINE AND EGG SAUCE

melt 4 tablespoons butter and blend in 4 tablespoons flour and 1/4 tablespoon dry mustard. cook for 1 minute and gradually stir in 2 cups milk, cook-stir about 5 minutes or until sauce is thick. add 4 hard-cooked eggs, finely chopped, 1/2 teaspoon salt, a little pepper, and 1/2 teaspoon Worcestershire sauce. stir in 1/2 cup dry white wine

(yields 4 servings)

STUFFINGS

Stuffings play an important part in seafood cooking. They are not difficult to prepare, can be used to fill all the little pockets and crevices so prevalent in fish and shellfish, to sop up and hold the flavors and juices released by cooking, and to make a modest-sized fish serve a multitude of eaters.

Stuffings may be dry or moist. Control the degree of moistness desired by mixing in 1/4 cup (more or less) of milk, clam broth, or fish stock. The recipes that follow will yield enough stuffing for a 4-pound fish. Use half the ingredients to stuff a small fish.

BASIC BREAD STUFFING

sauté 1 medium minced onion in 1/4 cup butter for 5 minutes or until light brown. remove from heat and blend in 1 teaspoon salt, a pinch of pepper, a pinch of thyme, and a pinch of rosemary. mix well with 2 cups fresh breadcrumbs. moisten to desired consistency with milk or fish stock

CAPER STUFFING

to basic stuffing add 2 tablespoons chopped capers and 1 chopped small sour pickle

CELERY STUFFING

to basic stuffing add 1 cup finely chopped raw celery

CHEESE STUFFING

to basic stuffing add 1 cup grated Cheshire or other mild cheese

CHESTNUT STUFFING

to basic stuffing add 1 cup finely chopped raw chestnuts

GREEN PEPPER STUFFING

to basic stuffing add 1/2 cup minced raw green pepper

HERB STUFFING

to basic stuffing add a little of the following herb combinations: chopped fresh dill, chopped fresh parsley, basil, minced capers or sage, celery salt, and marjoram or sage and basil or marjoram, thyme, and rosemary

SALT PORK HERB STUFFING

brown 1/2 cup chopped salt pork until crisp and blend in with basic stuffing, add 1 well-beaten egg, a pinch of nutmeg, and a tablespoon chopped parsley

MUSHROOM STUFFING

to basic stuffing add 1/2 cup minced mushrooms that have been sautéed in butter for 2 minutes

CRABMEAT STUFFING

sauté 1 medium minced onion in 1/4 cup butter until golden, with 1 teaspoon salt and a pinch of thyme, basil, paprika, and pepper. blend this mixture well with 2 cups fresh bread crumbs, a well-beaten egg and 1 cup cooked crabmeat. moisten, if desired, with fish stock or clam broth

CLAM STUFFING

follow recipe for crabmeat stuffing, substituting 1 cup drained chopped raw clams for the crabmeat

FLAKED FISH STUFFING

follow recipe for crabmeat stuffing, substituting 1 cup flaked cooked haddock, flounder, cod (or almost any other) for the crabmeat

LOBSTER STUFFING

follow recipe for crabmeat stuffing, substituting 1 cup minced cooked lobster meat for the crabmeat (variation: add 1 teaspoon sherry wine)

OYSTER STUFFING

follow recipe for crabmeat stuffing, substituting 1 cup drained chopped raw oysters for the crabmeat

SHRIMP STUFFING

follow recipe for crabmeat stuffing, substituting 1 cup minced cooked shrimp for the crabmeat

INDEX

Abalone, 12, 61–63
  abalone chowder, 45
  in casserole, 62
  fried, *see* Fried abalone
Abalone steaks
  au beurre noir, 63
  pan-broiled, 63
A la meunière cooking, 24
Alaskan king crab, 61, 82
Anchovies, 32
  anchovy toast, 28
Anchovy butter sauce, 195
  recipes calling for, 71, 110, 159
Anchovy mayonnaise, 194
Appetizers, 28–33, 92, 177–79

Baked cod with oyster stuffing, 80
Baked mullet
  au gratin, 111
  mullet, Mornay sauce, 111
Baked pike with sour cream, 121
Baked rockfish, Newburg, 133
Baked scallops with mushrooms,
    136
Baked shad
  in paper bag, 137
  shad, celery stuffing, 141
Baked weakfish, egg sauce, 171
Baking fish, general rules for, 22,
    24
Basic bread stuffing, 201–2
Basic white sauce, *see* Béchamel
    sauce
Bass, 23, 64–66, 148
  fresh-water, camp style, 64
  See also Sea bass; Striped bass
Béarnaise sauce, 195
Béchamel sauce, 193
  recipes calling for, 89, 99, 105,
    113, 138, 144, 180
Beurre noir, 195
  recipes calling for, 63, 74
Bisques, 51–54
  defined, 33
Black sea bass, 64, 108, 170

  with olive sauce, 66
Bloaters, pan-fried, 183
Blowfish, 12, 67, 148
Blue crab, 13, 83, 85
Bluefish, 60, 65, 68
  in bouillabaisse, 57
  with caper stuffing, 69
  shrimp-stuffed, 68
Boiled lobster, 103
Boston clam chowder, 48
Bouillabaisse, 55–57, 91
  defined, 33
  #1, 55
  #2, 56
  #3, 57
Bouquet garni, 39
Bread stuffing, *see* Stuffings
Brill, characteristics of, 94
Broiled eels with dill, 92
Broiled lobster, 104
Broiled striped bass maître
    d'hôtel, 65
Broiling, general rules for, 22, 24
Burgundy sauce, 196
Butterfish, 12, 148
  sautéed, 69

California halibut roast, 100
Canapés, *see* Appetizers
Caper sauce, 196
Caper stuffing, 69, 202
Carp, 26, 70–71, 179
  in burgundy, 71
  for gefilte fish, 181
  sautéed, with sauterne, 70
  See also Whitefish
Catfish, 72–76
  au beurre noir, 74
  Creole, 76
  curried, 72
  en papillote, 75
  sour, 73
  with shrimp sauce, 73
Catfish steaks, 73, 75–76, 99
  with mint, 76

Cauliflower for planked fish, 26, 126
Caviar, 175
Cebiche, 176
Celery sauce, 193
Celery stuffing, 202
    recipes calling for, 141, 174
Champagne sauce, 197
Charleston fish chowder, 47
Charleston oyster soup, 39
Cheddar-tuna canapés, 33
Cheese stuffing, 202
Chesapeake Bay crab cakes, 85
Chestnut stuffing, 202
Chicken for clambake, 79
Chicken halibut, 94, 97
Chowders, 45–50
    defined, 33
Cisco, 76
Clam belly soup, 34
Clam bisque
    oyster or, 51
    quick tomato and, 51
Clam broth, 34
    recipes calling for, 43, 51, 55, 133, 203
Clam chowder
    Boston, 48
    Manhattan, 46
    New England, 46
Clam stew, 41–44
    au naturel, 43
    Grand Central bar, 43
    Grand Central bar clam pan roast, 43
    old-fashioned, 41
    soft, 44
Clambake
    landlubber style, 79
    New England style, 78
Clams, 12, 77–79, 116, 119
    in bouillabaisse, 55
    casino, 177
    clam spread, 28
    clam stuffing, 201

deep-fat fried soft, 23
definition of hard and soft, 77
in Florida fish stew, 58
shucking hard-shell, 18
steamed, 24–25, 78
Cockles, 61, 77
Cocktail sauce, 32, 196
Cod (codfish), 68, 80–82, 97, 122, 183, 203
    baked, with oyster stuffing, 80
    in bouillabaisse, 55–56
    characteristics of, 22, 61
    cod cheeks and tongues madrilène, 178
    codfish cakes, 177
    codfish stew, 45
    in New England chowder, 46
    See also Salt cod; Scrod
Cod steaks (codfish steaks), 76, 100, 163
    in cream, 81
    curried, 82
Cold shrimp soup, 37
Conch (whelk), 12, 172
Coquilles St. Jacques, 178
Corn for clambake, 79
Court-bouillon, 25, 189–91
    fish stock made with, 192
    #1, 191
    #2, 190
    #3, 190
    #4, 190
    #5, 191
    recipes calling for, 75, 92, 97, 123, 132, 151, 167, 174
Crab (crabmeat), 82–88, 145
    in coquilles, 178
    crab cakes, Chesapeake Bay, 85
    crab Cioppino, 85
    crabmeat curry, 86
    crabmeat stuffing, 203
    creamed, 88
    deviled, 84

Crab (crabmeat) (*cont'd*)
general rules for preparing, 24–25
imperial, 84
mushroom and crab casserole, 88
steamed, 24–25, 86–87
in stuffed pompano, 124–25
See also Soft-shell crabs
Crab canapés, 28–32
crab Louis, 29
crabmeat balls, 28
hot buttered crabmeat, 29
Crab soup, 35–36, 37
with beer, 35
bisque à la Rector, 53
crab in bouillabaisse, 55
crab in seafood bisque, 54
Delaware, 35
gumbo, 60
"she," 35
soft-shell, 37
Crabs, 61
cleaning, 18
how to buy, 12, 14
Crappie, 23, 64
Crawfish, 89–90, 102
crawfish bisque, 52
crawfish, Nantua, 89–90
Creamed crabmeat, 88
Creamed oysters, 117
Croakers, 90, 148, 171
Curried catfish, 72
Curried codfish steaks, 82
Curried halibut casserole, 99
Curried mussels, 113
Curry sauce, 193
recipes calling for, 109, 159, 180

Dab, 12, 25
characteristics of, 94, 149
Deep-fried brandied eels, 93
Delaware crab soup, 35
Deviled crabs, 84

Deviled rockfish, 132
Deviled sardines, 32
Dijonnaise sauce, 161, 169
Dips, *see* Appetizers
Dover sole, characteristics of, 93, 149
Drawn butter, 168–69
Dungeness crab, 13, 83

Eels, 91–93
in bouillabaisse, 55, 57
broiled, with dill, 92
in herb sauce, 29
in marmite bretonne, 58
Eels, fried
deep-fried brandied, 93
fried elvers, 179
marinated, 93
Egg sauce, 165, 171
recipes calling for, 132, 145
Elvers, fried, 179
English sole, *see* Dover sole

Fillets of sole, 149–59
ambassadrice, 158
ancienne, 158
Argenteuil, 158
bonne femme, 156
Coquelin, 158
Dieppoise, 157
Duglère, 150
grand duc, 159
hongroise, 159
Hungarian style, 158
Marguéry, 151
Marinière, 154
Meunière, 154
Mirabeau, 159
Mornay, 153
Newburg, 159
oriental, 159
Orly, 150
Oysters, 156
Persian, 159
Provençale, 153

Fillets of sole (*cont'd*)
  Shrimp, 155
  véronique, 151
  Vermouth, 152
  Walewska, 159
  in white wine, 157
Finnan haddie, 80
  finnan haddie snacks, 30
  in milk, 96
Fish fillets, 73, 110, 111, 149,
      151, 159
  for crab soup, 37
  cutting, 17
  in fish chowders, 47, 49
  general rules for preparing,
      22–24, 25
  haddock, 96
  how to buy, 13–14
  poached in court-bouillon, 25,
      189
  pompano, 123–24
  rockfish, 102–7
  See also Fillets of sole; Shad
      fillets
Fish fumet, *see* Fumet
Fish mousse, 26, 154–56
  garnishes for, 155
  sauces for, 156
Fish roe, 187
  shad roe with bacon, 187
Fish steaks, 66, 108–9, 111
  cutting, 16
  general rules for preparing,
      24–26
  halibut, 81, 98–100
  how to buy, 13–14
  See also Abalone steaks; Cat-
      fish steaks; Cod steaks;
      Grouper steaks; Lingcod
      steaks; Mackerel steaks;
      Pollock steaks; Swordfish
      steaks; Tuna steaks
Fish sticks
  cutting, 17
  deep-fat fried, 22–23

how to buy, 14
Fish stock, 189
  in fumet, 190
  #1, 189
  #2, #3, #4, #5, #6, 190
  recipes calling for, 31, 53,
      55–57, 68, 89, 100,
      108–9, 114, 118, 138,
      169, 174
Flaked fish stuffing, 174
Flaked rockfish
  béchamel, 113
  as canapé, 31
Flatfish, 93–100
  characteristics of, 94
  how to buy, 12
  See also Dab; Flounder; Hali-
      but; Sole; Turbot
Florida fish stew, 58
Flounder, 94, 149, 203
  characteristics of, 61, 94, 149
  general rules for preparing, 22,
      25–26
  how to buy, 12
  in marmite bretonne, 58
  See also Haddock
  See also Sole
Fluke, 12, 94
  characteristics of, 94, 149
Forcemeats
  for fish mousse, 179
  how to prepare, 26
French dressing (vinaigrette
      sauce), 108, 199
Fresh-water bass, camp style, 64
Fried abalone, 62
  deep-fat, 23
Fried elvers, 179
Fried halibut bits, 98
Fried marinated eels, 92
Fried mussels, 113
Fried shrimp, 143
  deep-fat, 22–23
Fried whitebait, 173
Frog, 180

Frogs' legs
  à l'anglaise, 181
  à la Horsher, 181
  Provençale, 180
Frying methods
  deep-fat frying, 23–24
  pan frying, 23
Fumet, 192
  basting with, 61
  poaching fish in, 25
  recipes calling for, 58, 71, 100,
      130, 158, 199

Garnishes for fish mousse, 180
Gefilte fish, 174, 181
Germaine sauce, 197
Golden broiled shad fillets, 140
Golden brown blowfish, 67
Grand Central bar oyster (or
      clam) stew, 42
  oyster (or clam) pan roast, 43
Gravlax, 182
Gray sole, 12, 94, 176
  characteristics of, 93–94, 149
Grayling, 95
Green mayonnaise, 195
Green pepper stuffing, 202
Grilled mullet, anchovy butter
      sauce, 110
Grilling, general rules for, 22, 24
Grouper (ocean perch), 12, 95,
      120, 149
Grouper steaks, 66, 108, 129,
      176
  grilled, 95
Gulf flounder, 94
Gumbos, 59–60
  defined, 33

Haddock, 68, 96, 149, 201
  in bouillabaisse, 58
  characteristics of, 22, 89
  for crab soup, 37
  haddock fillets, mushroom
      sauce, 96

in marmite bretonne, 58
in New England chowder, 48
scalloped, au gratin, 96
See also Finnan haddie
Hake, *see* Whiting
Halibut, 22, 97–100
  à la diable, 98
  à la poulette, 99
  California halibut roast, 100
  characteristics of, 94
  curried halibut casserole, 99
  fried bits of, 98
  halibut steaks, 81–82, 98–100
Herb sauce, 193
  herb mayonnaise, 194
Herb stuffing, 202
  salt pork, 174, 201
  whitefish with, 174
Herring, 32
  about, 76, 91, 100–1, 183
  herring dip, 30
  See also Kippers; Lingcod
      steaks; Sardine canapés;
      Whitebait
Hollandaise sauce, 197–98
  recipes calling for, 89–90, 105,
      123, 196
Hors d'oeuvres, *see* Appetizers
Horseradish-marmalade   sauce,
      143, 198
Horseradish sauce, 198
Hot buttered crabmeat canapés,
      29
Hot lobster canapés, 31

Imperial crab, 84
Indienne sauce, 195

Kingfish (king mackerel) steak
      vinaigrette, 108
Kippers, 100–1, 183
  kipper snacks, 30

Lemon sole, 12, 94
  characteristics of, 94, 149

Lingcod steaks, 81, 99–101, 163
  steaks, mushroom stuffing, 101
Lobster, 24–25, 86, 102–6, 145
  à la Américaine, 107
  boiled, 104
  broiled, 103
  in clambakes, 78–79
  in coquilles, 178
  in fillets of sole, Walewska, 159
  lobster sauce, *see* Shrimp (or
      lobster) sauce
  lobster stuffing, 203
  Newburg, 105
  steamed, 24–25, 102
  stuffed, 104
  Thermidor, 106
Lobster canapés, 30–31
  hot, 31
  lobster spread, 30
Lobster soups, 36
  bisque, 53
  chowder, 49
  gumbo, 59
  lobster in bouillabaisse, 55–57
  lobster in fish stew, 58
Lobsters, 61
  cleaning, 18
  how to buy, 12, 14

Mackerel, 22, 61, 65, 108
Mackerel steaks, 66, 170
  kingfish steak vinaigrette, 108
  steak, curry sauce, 109
Maine scrod chowder, 50
Maître d'hôtel sauce, 198
  recipes calling for, 65, 180
Manhattan clam chowder, 46
Marinated mullet fillets, 110
Marmite bretonne, 58
Mayonnaise, 194
  recipes calling for, 32, 98
Mayonnaise sauces, 194–95
Mexican pan-broiled shrimp, 146
Mornay sauce, 194
  recipes calling for, 111, 159

Mullet, 109–11
  baked, *see* Baked mullet
  in bouillabaisse, 55
  grilled, anchovy butter sauce,
      110
  marinated fillets of, 110
Mushroom and crab casserole, 88
Mushroom sauce, 96, 193
Mushroom stuffing, 203
  recipes calling for, 65, 101, 174
Muskellunge steaks, 100
Mussels, 12, 25, 112–13
  in bouillabaisse, 55
  cleaning, 18–19
  curried, 113
  in fillets of sole, Marguéry, 151
  fried, 113
  garnishing fish mousse, 180
  hongroise, 113
  marinière, 112
  mussel soup, 38
  mussel tidbits, 31
  Provençale, 113
Mustard sauce
  mustard mayonnaise, 195
  recipe calling for, 182

New England clam chowder, 46
New England fish chowder, 49
New Orleans oyster soup, 40
New Orleans shrimp (or crab)
      gumbo, 60
Newburg sauce, 197
  recipes calling for, 105, 117,
      133, 159
Normandie sauce, 199
  recipes calling for, 67, 158, 180

Octopus, 162
  characteristics of, 160
  cleaning, 19
Okra gumbos, *see* Gumbos
Old-fashioned oyster (or clam)
      stew, 41
Old-fashioned scallop broil, 137

Oyster crab, 82–83
Oyster soup
  belgique, 39
  bisque, 51
  Charleston, 39
  New Orleans, 40
  oyster gumbo filé, 59
  oysters in bouillabaisse, 55
  Rhode Island chowder, 50
  velouté, 40
Oyster stew, 42–43
  Grand Central bar, 45
  Grand Central bar oyster pan
      roast, 43
  old-fashioned, 41
Oyster stuffing, 80, 201
Oysters, 25, 114–20, 145
  à la King, 116
  à la Newburg, 117
  au gratin, 117
  creamed, 117
  en brochette, 118
  in fillets of sole, Marguéry, 151
  garnishing fish mousse, 180
  grande dame, 118
  how to buy, 12, 14
  Rockefeller, 185
  St. Pierre, 119
  scalloped, 120
  shucking, 17
Oysters, fried
  deep-fat fried, 22–23
  oyster fritters, 119
  oyster fry, 115

Pan-broiled abalone steaks, 63
Pan-broiled shad fillets, sauterne,
    140
Pan-fried bloaters, 183
Pan-fried scup fillets, 128
Pan-fried smelt, 148
Perch, 22, 64, 120
  ocean, *see* Grouper
Pike, 26, 121, 179
  baked, with sour cream, 121

  for gefilte fish, 181
Planked pompano, 126
Planking, general rules for, 22, 26
Poached pollock steaks, 123
Poached trout with shallots, 167
Poaching, 189
  general rules for, 22, 25
Pollock, 68, 80, 122–23
  savory baked, 122
Pollock steaks, 76
  poached, 123
Pompano, 123–26
  in Florida fish stew, 58
  planked, 126
  stuffed, en papillote (Mont-
      golfier), 124
Porgy (scup), 12, 127–28
  Charleston style, 127
  pan-fried scup fillets, 128
Potatoes, mashed
  for codfish cakes, 177
  for planked fish, 26, 126
Prawns, 12, 142
  cleaning, 18
  deep-fat fried, 23
Provençale sauce, 199

Quick clam and tomato bisque,
    51

Rainbow trout en papillote, 168
Ravigote sauce, 199
  recipes calling for, 67, 150,
      180
Red snapper, 61, 68, 129–31
  à l'orange, 130
  in bouillabaisse, 56
  Caribe style, 131
  in crab soup, 37
  in marmite bretonne, 58
  red snapper steak, Gulf style,
      129
Rémoulade sauce, 199
Rhode Island oyster chowder, 50
Rock (spiny) lobster, 102–3, 106

Rockfish, 12, 65, 132–33
  baked, Newburg, 133
  deviled, 132
  parisienne, 132
  See also Flaked rockfish;
      Striped bass
Rusty dab, 94

Salmon, 22, 91, 134
  for gravlax, 182
  salmon steaks, 81, 99
  salmon steak, parmesan, 134
  Seattle salmon steak, 135
  smoked, 32
Salt cod, 177
  Provençale, 184
Salt herring, 100–1
Salt pork herb stuffing, 174, 201
Sardine canapés, 30
  deviled sardines, 32
  sardine snacks, 32
Sauce verte, 195
Sauces, 32, 73, 96, 107–11, 143,
      150–59, 160, 177–80,
      184–85, 192–99
  about, 14, 26, 61, 67, 83
  for fish mousse, 180
  for hors d'oeuvres platter, 32
  marinière, 112
  mayonnaise, 194–95
  olive, sea bass with, 66
  See also Béchamel sauce;
      Beurre noir; Egg sauce;
      Hollandaise sauce; Maître
      d'hôtel sauce; Newburg
      sauce; Sauterne sauce;
      Velouté sauce
Sautéed butterfish, 69
Sautéed carp with sauterne, 70
Sautéeing, steps to follow in, 24
Sauterne sauce, 200
  recipes calling for, 140, 158,
      174
Savory baked pollock, 122
Scaling fish, 16

Scalloped haddock au gratin, 96
Scalloped oysters, 120
Scallops, 12, 136–38
  baked, with mushrooms, 138
  coquilles St. Jacques, 178
  deep-fat fried sea or bay, 22–
      23
  en brochette, 137
  fry, 136
  old-fashioned scallop broil, 137
  scallop stew, 44
  in the raw, 189
  in wine, 138
Scrod, 80
  Maine scrod chowder, 50
Scup, *see* Porgy
Sea bass, 22, 121
  in bouillabaisse, 56
  in marmite bretonne, 58
  See also Black sea bass
Sea squab (blowfish), 12, 67, 148
Sea urchins, 12, 139
Seafood
  general rules for preparing,
      22–26
  how to buy, 12–14
  how to clean and dress, 16–19
Seafood bisque, 54
Seafood hors d'oeuvres platter, 32
Seafood Paella, 186
Shad, 65, 139–41
  about, 22, 91
  baked, *see* Baked shad
Shad fillets, broiled
  golden broiled, 140
  pan-broiled, sauterne, 140
"She" crab soup, 35
Sheepshead, 142
Shellfish
  how to buy, 12–14
  varieties of, 60–61; *see also*
      Clams; Crab; Lobster;
      Mussels; Oysters; Prawns;
      Scallops; Shrimp; Whelk

Shrimp, 31, 86, 89, 142–47
  au gratin, 143
  cleaning, 18
  in coquilles, 178
  in fillets of sole, Marguéry, 151
  fried, *see* Fried shrimp
  garnishing fish mousse, 179
  general rules for preparing, 22–26
  in Gulf style red snapper steak, 129
  how to buy, 12, 14
  Mexican pan-broiled, 146
  New Orleans, 144
  pilau, 146
  shrimp canapés, 30–33
  shrimp curry, 147
  shrimp patties, 144
  shrimp pie, 145
  shrimp-stuffed bluefish, 68
  shrimp stuffing, 204
  shrimps Louisiana, 145
  in stuffed pompano, 124–25
  tangy steamed, 147
  in truites farcies, 168–69
Shrimp (or lobster) sauce, 200
  recipes calling for, 73, 180
Shrimp soups, 37–38
  bisque, 54
  chowder, 49
  cold, 37
  gumbo, 60
  shrimp in bouillabaisse, 55
  shrimp in seafood bisque, 54
  stew, 44
Smelt, 13, 148
  deep-fat fried, 23
  pan-fried, 148
Smoked salmon, 32
Snacks, *see* Appetizers
Snails and periwinkles, 187–88
  snail butter, 188
  snails Provençale, 188
Snapper soup, 164
Snapper stew, 166

Soft clam stew, 44
Soft-shell crabs
  cleaning, 18
  crab soup, 37
  described, 82
  fried, 87
Sole, 12, 94, 149–59, 176
  characteristics of, 94
  fillets of, *see* Fillets of sole
  general rules for preparing, 25–26
Soups, 33–40, 164
  defined, 33
  See also Bisques; Bouillabaisse;
      Court-bouillon; Chowders;
      Fish stock; Fumet; Stews
Sour catfish, 73
Spiny lobster, 102–4, 106
Squid, 160–62
  in bouillabaisse, 56
  characteristics of, 61, 160
  cleaning, 19
  in "ink," 162
  stuffed, 161
Starry flounder, 12, 94, 149
Steamed clams, 24–25, 78
Steamed lobster, 24–25, 103
Steamed shrimp, 147
Steaming, general rules for, 22, 24–25
Stews, 41–45, 55–57, 91
  defined, 41
  snapper, 166
  See also Bouillabaisse; Soups
Stock, *see* Fish stock
Stone crab, 61, 83
Striped bass, 64–65
  in bouillabaisse, 56
  broiled, maître d'hôtel, 65
  with mushroom stuffing, 65
  See also Rockfish
Stuffed lobster, 104
Stuffed pompano en papillote, 124–25
Stuffed squid, 161

Stuffed trout, 169
Stuffings, 14, 68, 80, 141, 201–4
  for crawfish bisque, 52
  for whitefish, 174
  See also Forcemeats; Mush-
    room stuffing
Summer flounder, *see* Fluke
Swordfish, 61, 163
Swordfish steaks, 81–82, 99–100
  with mushrooms, 163

Tangy steamed shrimp, 147
Tartar sauce, 200
  recipes calling for, 32, 143
Terrapin, 61, 164–66
  cleaning, 19
Terrapin à la Maryland, 164–66
  #1, 164–65
  #2, 165–66
  #3, 166
Tomato and clam bisque, 51
Tomato mayonnaise, 195
Trout, 61, 64–65, 95, 148, 167–
    69
  general rules for preparing,
    22, 26
  poached, with shallots, 167
  rainbow, en papillote, 168
  Truites farcies (stuffed), 168–
    69
Truite au bleu, 188
Tuna, 61
Tuna canapés, 28, 30–33
  cheddar-tuna, 33
Tuna steaks, 66, 108, 170

  royale, 170
Turbot, 25
  au champagne, 97
  characteristics of, 94
Turtle, 61, 164–66
  cleaning, 19
  snapper stew, 166

Velouté sauce, 200
  recipes calling for, 97, 150,
    158, 168, 178, 180, 198
Vinaigrette sauce, 108, 201

Weakfish, baked, egg sauce, 171
Whale, 172
Whelk (conch), 12, 172
White sauce, *see* Béchamel sauce
White wine and egg sauce, 201
  recipes calling for, 132, 180
Whitebait, 12, 173, 188
  deep-fat fried, 23
  fried, 173
  and oyster crabs, 188
Whitefish, 70, 174
  for gefilte fish, 174, 179
  with herb stuffing, 174
  with sauterne sauce, 174
Whiting (hake), 175, 179
  about, 26, 97
  à la Bercy, 175
  in bouillabaisse, 55
  in crab soup, 37
  in marmite bretonne, 58
Winter flounder, 12
  characteristics of, 94, 149

SPECIES OF SEAFOOD	RELATIVE SIZE					FAT CONTENT	
	VERY LARGE	LARGE	MEDIUM	SMALL	VERY SMALL	HIGH	LOW
*oyster			●	●	●		●
perch			●	●		●	
*periwinkle					●		●
pickerel			●	●			●
pike		●	●				●
plaice		●	●	●			●
pollock	●	●	●				●
pompano			●	●		●	
porgy (scup)			●	●			●
red snapper			●	●		●	
rockfish (striped bass)		●	●			●	
salmon	●	●	●				●
sardine				●	●		●
*scallop			●	●			●
*sea urchin				●			●
shad			●			●	
sheepshead			●				●
*shrimp, prawn		●	●	●	●		●
smelt				●	●	●	
*snail				●			●
sole			●				●
spot				●	●		●
sprat (brisling)					●	●	
*squid				●	●		●
swordfish	●	●					●
*terrapin, turtle			●	●			●
trout			●	●		●	
tuna, albacore, bonito	●	●				●	
turbot		●					●
weakfish (sea trout)				●			●
whale	●					●	
*whelk (conch)			●				●
whitebait					●	●	
whitefish (chub)			●			●	
whiting				●		●	

*shellfish   O occasionally